First Course
Graded Exercises
Second Edition

Bryan Coombs

Pitman

PITMAN PUBLISHING LIMITED
128 Long Acre, London, WC2E 9AN

Associated Companies
Pitman Publishing Pty Ltd, Melbourne
Pitman Publishing New Zealand Ltd, Wellington

© Pitman Publishing Limited 1982

First edition 1977
Second edition 1982
Reprinted 1982, 1983, 1984

Printed in Great Britain at The Pitman Press, Bath

ISBN 0 273 01807 8

PUBLISHER'S PREFACE

Pitman 2000 First Course Graded Exercises (Second Edition), is produced for the purposes of intensive reading, re-reading and writing practice in sentence form on a page for page basis with *Pitman 2000 First Course* (Second Edition).

Provision has been made at the end of each exercise for the reading times to be noted. Any outlines that caused hesitation in the first and second readings should be drilled so that the third and final reading shows a marked increase in the reading rate.

The material in this book is clearly marked with the relevant page numbers in *Pitman 2000 First Course* (Second Edition) and it includes additional revisionary drills of short forms and phrases presented as continuous material of up to 180 words in length. These longer passages are intended to provide graded theory material for early speed development.

As an aid to increasing your transcription speed seven additional transcription practice pieces are included at the end of this book. Read each piece as quickly as possible, then write it from dictation and transcribe your own notes on to the typewriter.

INDEX

UNIT 1 (Page 4, First Course)

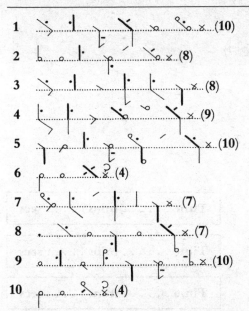

1 Read the above sentences, noting how long it takes you. If you cannot read any outline check with the key.

> Time . . . . . . mins . . . . . secs

2 Repeat the reading exercise, aiming to increase your reading speed. Note your timing.

> Time . . . . . . mins . . . . . secs

3 Drill all outlines which caused you any hesitancy in the last reading. Now repeat the reading, aiming to read the short-hand as quickly as if the material was typewritten.

> Time . . . . . . mins . . . . . secs

UNIT 1 Short Form and Phrase Drill

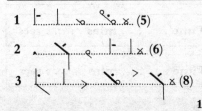

1

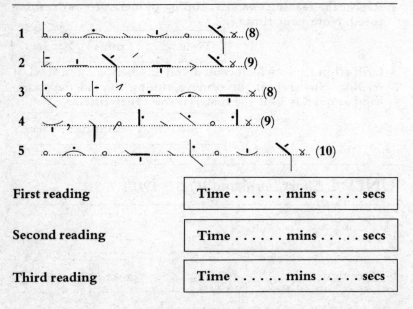

4 (4)

5 (5)

6 (7)

7 (4)

8 (7)

9 (7)

10 (7)

First reading	Time . . . . . . mins . . . . . secs
Second reading	Time . . . . . . mins . . . . . secs
Third reading	Time . . . . . . mins . . . . . secs

UNIT 2 *(Page 6, First Course)*

1 (8)

2 (9)

3 (8)

4 (9)

5 (10)

First reading	Time . . . . . . mins . . . . . secs
Second reading	Time . . . . . . mins . . . . . secs
Third reading	Time . . . . . . mins . . . . . secs

UNIT 2 (*Page 6, First Course*)

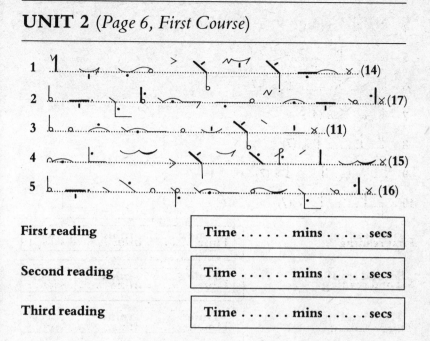

1 .... (14)

2 .... (17)

3 .... (11)

4 .... (15)

5 .... (16)

First reading	Time . . . . . . mins . . . . . secs
Second reading	Time . . . . . . mins . . . . . secs
Third reading	Time . . . . . . mins . . . . . secs

UNIT 2 *Short Form and Phrase Drill*

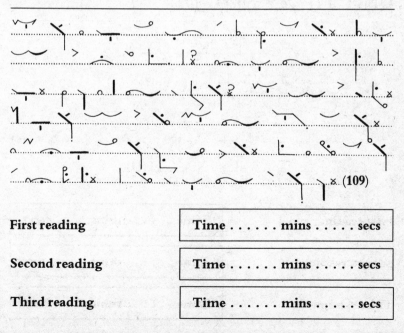

.... (109)

First reading	Time . . . . . . mins . . . . . secs
Second reading	Time . . . . . . mins . . . . . secs
Third reading	Time . . . . . . mins . . . . . secs

UNIT 3 *(Page 9, First Course)*

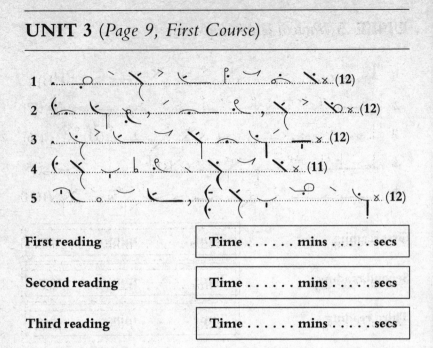

First reading	Time . . . . . . mins . . . . . secs
Second reading	Time . . . . . . mins . . . . secs
Third reading	Time . . . . . . mins . . . . secs

UNIT 3 *(Page 9, First Course)*

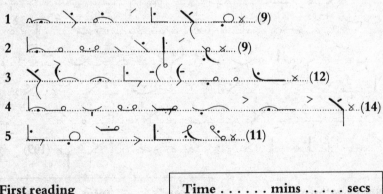

First reading	Time . . . . . . mins . . . . . secs
Second reading	Time . . . . . . mins . . . . . secs
Third reading	Time . . . . . . mins . . . . . secs

UNIT 3 *(Page 11, First Course)*

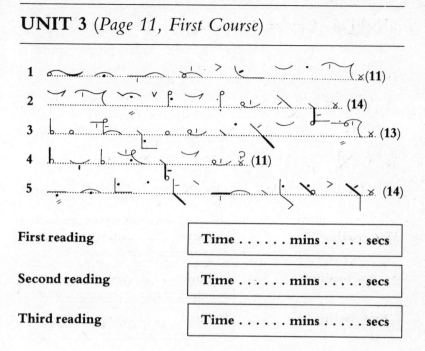

First reading   Time . . . . . . mins . . . . . secs

Second reading   Time . . . . . . mins . . . . . secs

Third reading   Time . . . . . . mins . . . . . secs

UNIT 3 *Short Form and Phrase Drill*

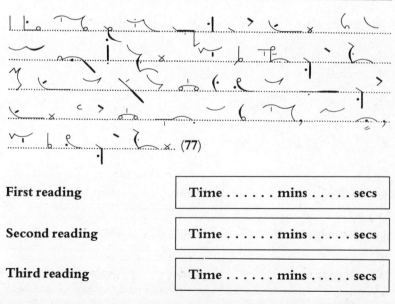

First reading   Time . . . . . . mins . . . . . secs

Second reading   Time . . . . . . mins . . . . . secs

Third reading   Time . . . . . . mins . . . . . secs

UNIT 4 (*Page 13, First Course*)

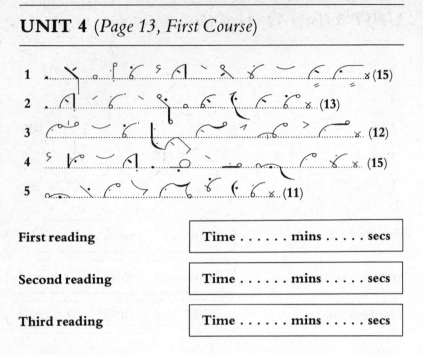

First reading	Time . . . . . . mins . . . . . secs
Second reading	Time . . . . . . mins . . . . . secs
Third reading	Time . . . . . . mins . . . . . secs

UNIT 4 (*Page 15, First Course*)

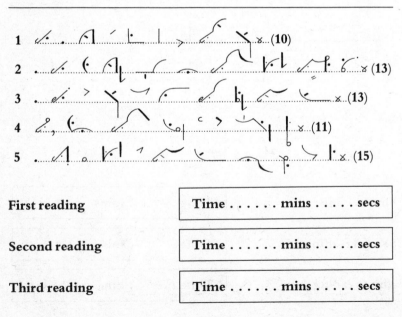

First reading	Time . . . . . . mins . . . . . secs
Second reading	Time . . . . . . mins . . . . . secs
Third reading	Time . . . . . . mins . . . . . secs

UNIT 4 *Short Form and Phrase Drill*

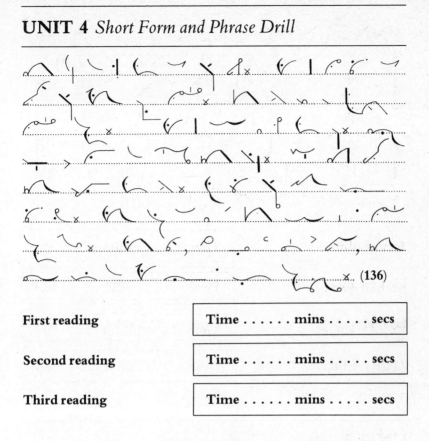

(136)

First reading	Time . . . . . mins . . . . . secs
Second reading	Time . . . . . mins . . . . . secs
Third reading	Time . . . . . mins . . . . . secs

UNIT 5 *(Page 18, First Course)*

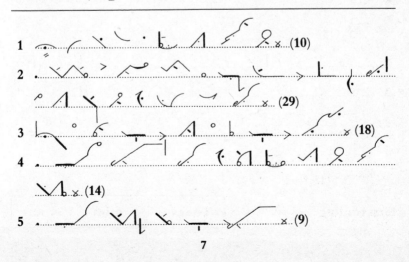

1 ... (10)

2 ... (29)

3 ... (18)

4 ... (14)

5 ... (9)

7

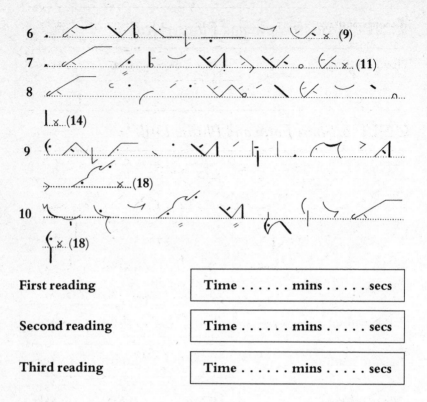

6 ..... **(9)**

7 ..... **(11)**

8 ..... **(14)**

9 ..... **(18)**

10 ..... **(18)**

First reading	Time . . . . . . mins . . . . . secs
Second reading	Time . . . . . . mins . . . . . secs
Third reading	Time . . . . . . mins . . . . . secs

UNIT 5 *(Page 19, First Course)*

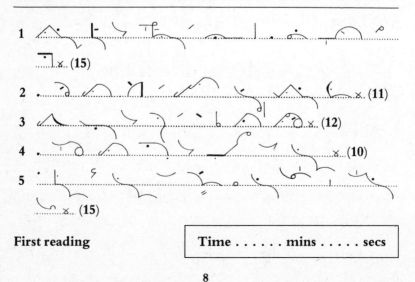

1 ..... **(15)**

2 ..... **(11)**

3 ..... **(12)**

4 ..... **(10)**

5 ..... **(15)**

First reading	Time . . . . . . mins . . . . . secs

UNIT 5 *Short Form and Phrase Drill*

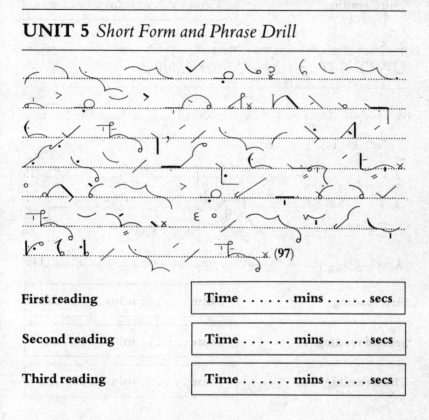

...×. (97)

First reading	Time . . . . . . mins . . . . . secs
Second reading	Time . . . . . . mins . . . . . secs
Third reading	Time . . . . . . mins . . . . . secs

UNIT 6 *(Page 23, First Course)*

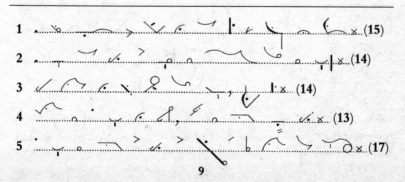

1 .... ×.(15)

2 .... ×.(14)

3 .... ×. (14)

4 .... ×. (13)

5 .... ×.(17)

9

First reading	Time . . . . . mins . . . . secs
Second reading	Time . . . . . mins . . . . secs
Third reading	Time . . . . . mins . . . . secs

UNIT 6 (*Pages 24–5, First Course*)

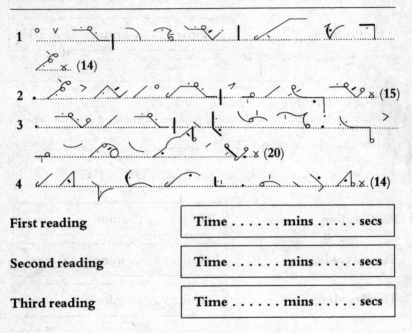

1 (14)

2 (15)

3 (20)

4 (14)

First reading	Time . . . . . mins . . . . secs
Second reading	Time . . . . . mins . . . . secs
Third reading	Time . . . . . mins . . . . secs

UNIT 6 *Short Form and Phrase Drill*

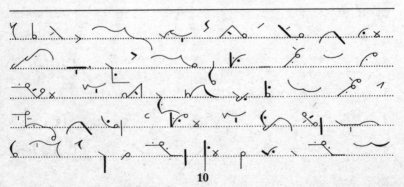

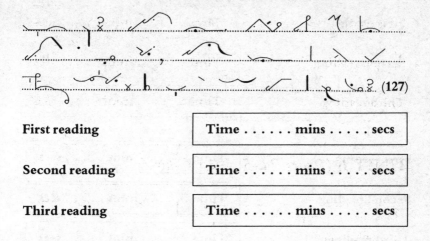

(127)

First reading	Time . . . . . . mins . . . . . secs
Second reading	Time . . . . . . mins . . . . . secs
Third reading	Time . . . . . . mins . . . . . secs

UNIT 7 (*Page 28, First Course*)

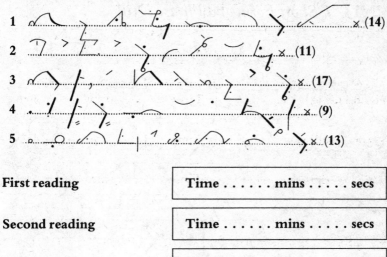

1 ... (14)
2 ... (11)
3 ... (17)
4 ... (9)
5 ... (13)

First reading	Time . . . . . . mins . . . . . secs
Second reading	Time . . . . . . mins . . . . . secs
Third reading	Time . . . . . . mins . . . . . secs

UNIT 7 (*Pages 28–30, First Course*)

1 ... (14)
2 ... (15)

3 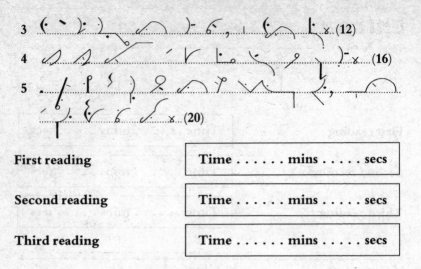 (12)

4 (16)

5 (20)

First reading | Time . . . . . . mins . . . . . secs

Second reading | Time . . . . . . mins . . . . . secs

Third reading | Time . . . . . . mins . . . . . secs

UNIT 7 *Short Form and Phrase Drill*

(141)

First reading | Time . . . . . . mins . . . . . secs

Second reading | Time . . . . . . mins . . . . . secs

Third reading | Time . . . . . . mins . . . . . secs

UNIT 8 *(Page 32, First Course)*

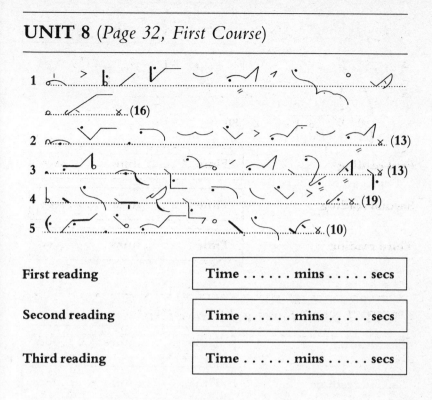

1 ...... (16)

2 ...... (13)

3 ...... (13)

4 ...... (19)

5 ...... (10)

First reading	Time . . . . . . mins . . . . . secs
Second reading	Time . . . . . . mins . . . . . secs
Third reading	Time . . . . . . mins . . . . . secs

UNIT 8 *(Page 33, First Course)*

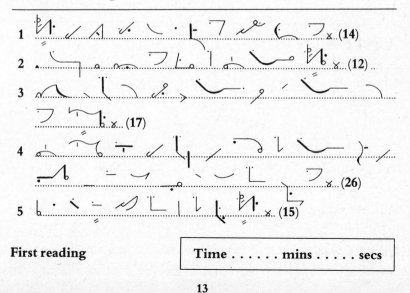

1 ...... (14)

2 ...... (12)

3 ...... (17)

4 ...... (26)

5 ...... (15)

First reading	Time . . . . . . mins . . . . . secs

Second reading

Time . . . . . . mins . . . . . secs

Third reading

Time . . . . . . mins . . . . . secs

UNIT 8 (*Page 34, First Course*)

1 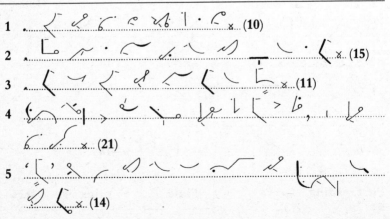 x. (10)

2 x. (10)

3 x. (10)

4 x. (12)

5 x (16)

First reading

Time . . . . . . mins . . . . . secs

Second reading

Time . . . . . . mins . . . . . secs

Third reading

Time . . . . . . mins . . . . . secs

UNIT 8 (*Pages 34–5, First Course*)

1 x. (10)

2 x. (15)

3 x. (11)

4 x. (21)

5 x. (14)

14

First reading	Time . . . . . . mins . . . . . secs
Second reading	Time . . . . . . mins . . . . . secs
Third reading	Time . . . . . . mins . . . . . secs

UNIT 8 *Short Form and Phrase Drill*

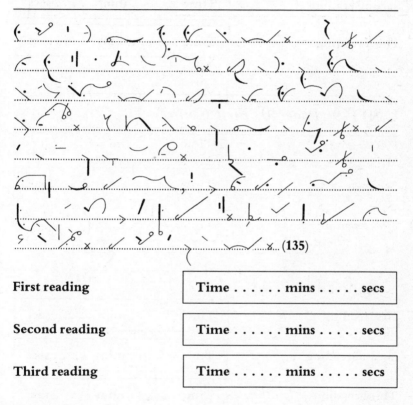

(135)

First reading	Time . . . . . . mins . . . . . secs
Second reading	Time . . . . . . mins . . . . . secs
Third reading	Time . . . . . . mins . . . . . secs

UNIT 9 *(Pages 38–40, First Course)*

1

(13)

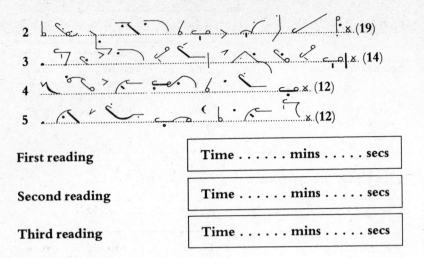

2 ... (19)
3 ... (14)
4 ... (12)
5 ... (12)

First reading	Time . . . . . . mins . . . . . secs
Second reading	Time . . . . . . mins . . . . . secs
Third reading	Time . . . . . . mins . . . . . secs

UNIT 9 (*Page 40, First Course*)

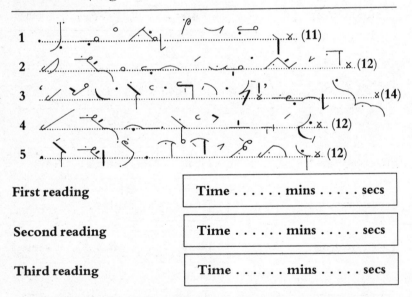

1 ... (11)
2 ... (12)
3 ... (14)
4 ... (12)
5 ... (12)

First reading	Time . . . . . . mins . . . . . secs
Second reading	Time . . . . . . mins . . . . . secs
Third reading	Time . . . . . . mins . . . . . secs

UNIT 9 *Short Form and Phrase Drill*

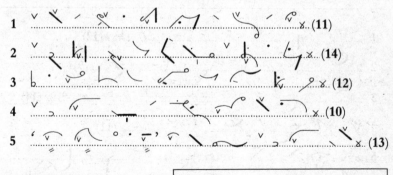

...(132)

First reading	Time . . . . . mins . . . . . secs
Second reading	Time . . . . . mins . . . . . secs
Third reading	Time . . . . . mins . . . . . secs

UNIT 10 (*Page 43, First Course*)

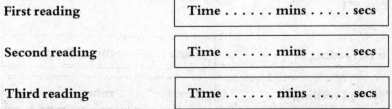

1 ...(11)
2 ...(14)
3 ...(12)
4 ...(10)
5 ...(13)

First reading	Time . . . . . mins . . . . . secs
Second reading	Time . . . . . mins . . . . . secs
Third reading	Time . . . . . mins . . . . . secs

UNIT 10 (*Pages 43–4, First Course*)

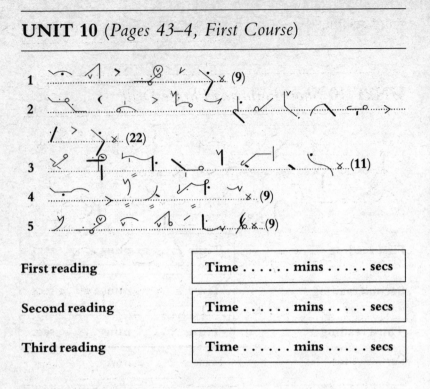

1 .... (9)

2 .... (22)

3 .... (11)

4 .... (9)

5 .... (9)

First reading	Time . . . . . . mins . . . . . secs
Second reading	Time . . . . . . mins . . . . . secs
Third reading	Time . . . . . . mins . . . . . secs

UNIT 10 (*Pages 44–5, First Course*)

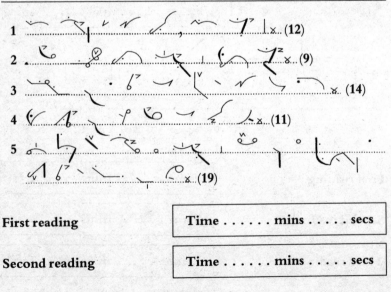

1 .... (12)

2 .... (9)

3 .... (14)

4 .... (11)

5 .... (19)

First reading	Time . . . . . . mins . . . . . secs
Second reading	Time . . . . . . mins . . . . . secs

UNIT 10 *Short Form and Phrase Drill*

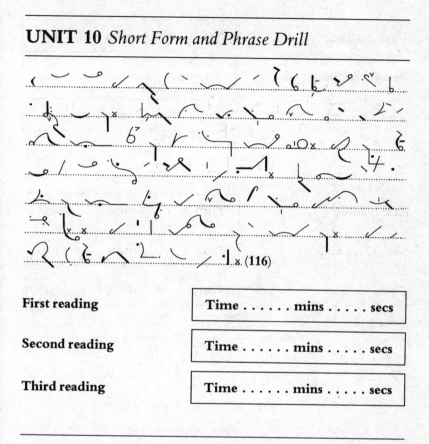

(116)

First reading

Time . . . . . . mins . . . . . secs

Second reading

Time . . . . . . mins . . . . . secs

Third reading

Time . . . . . . mins . . . . . secs

UNIT 11 *(Page 47, First Course)*

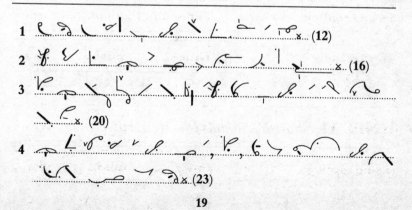

1   (12)

2   (16)

3   (20)

4   (23)

19

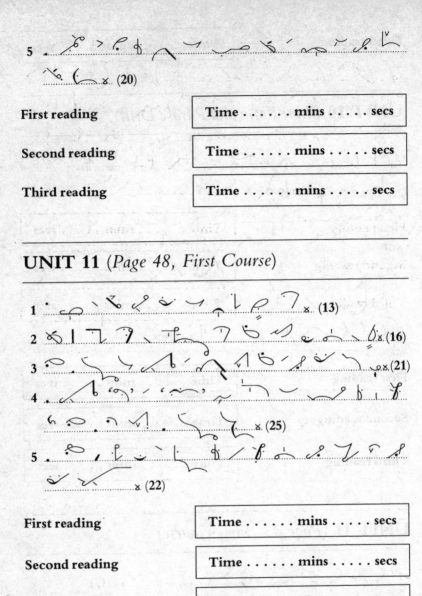

5 .... x. (20)

First reading	Time . . . . . . mins . . . . . secs
Second reading	Time . . . . . . mins . . . . . secs
Third reading	Time . . . . . . mins . . . . . secs

UNIT 11 (*Page 48, First Course*)

1 .... x. (13)

2 .... x. (16)

3 .... x. (21)

4 .... x. (25)

5 .... x. (22)

First reading	Time . . . . . . mins . . . . . secs
Second reading	Time . . . . . . mins . . . . . secs
Third reading	Time . . . . . . mins . . . . . secs

UNIT 11 *Short Form and Phrase Drill*

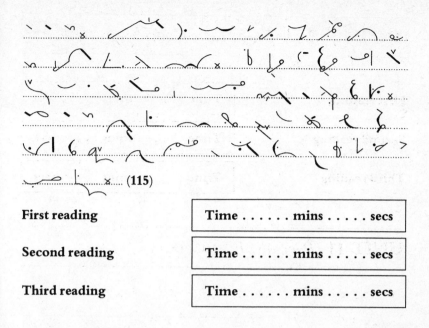

...... (115)

First reading

Time . . . . . mins . . . . . secs

Second reading

Time . . . . . mins . . . . . secs

Third reading

Time . . . . . mins . . . . . secs

UNIT 12 (*Page 52, First Course*)

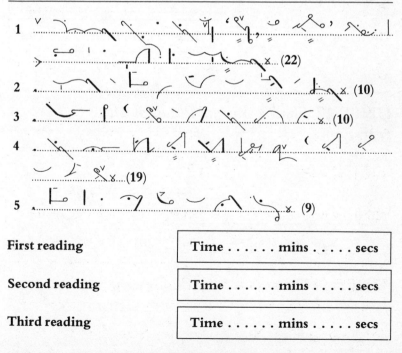

1 ...... (22)

2 ...... (10)

3 ...... (10)

4 ...... (19)

5 ...... (9)

First reading

Time . . . . . mins . . . . . secs

Second reading

Time . . . . . mins . . . . . secs

Third reading

Time . . . . . mins . . . . . secs

UNIT 12 *(Pages 54–5, First Course)*

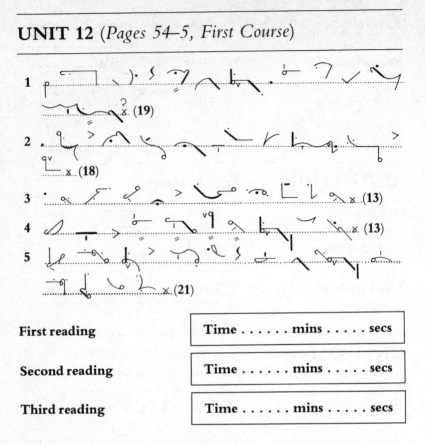

1 ... **(19)**

2 ... **(18)**

3 ... **(13)**

4 ... **(13)**

5 ... **(21)**

First reading	Time . . . . . . mins . . . . . secs
Second reading	Time . . . . . . mins . . . . . secs
Third reading	Time . . . . . . mins . . . . . secs

UNIT 12 *Short Form and Phrase Drill*

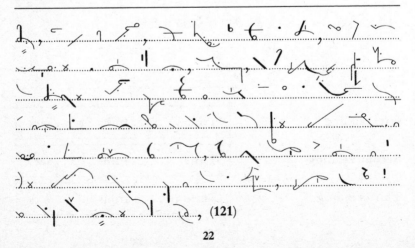

(121)

First reading	Time . . . . . mins . . . . . secs
Second reading	Time . . . . . mins . . . . . secs
Third reading	Time . . . . . mins . . . . . secs

UNIT 13 (*Page 57, First Course*)

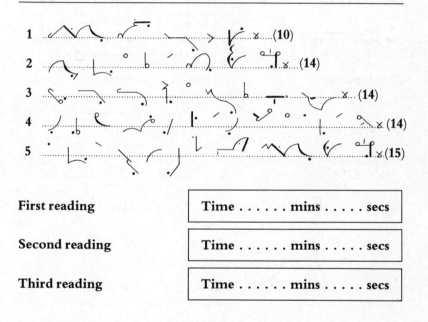

1 ....(10)
2 ....(14)
3 ....(14)
4 ....(14)
5 ....(15)

First reading	Time . . . . . mins . . . . . secs
Second reading	Time . . . . . mins . . . . . secs
Third reading	Time . . . . . mins . . . . . secs

UNIT 13 (*Page 58, First Course*)

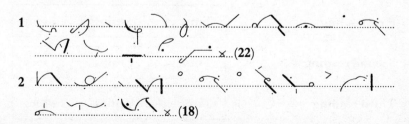

1 ....(22)
2 ....(18)

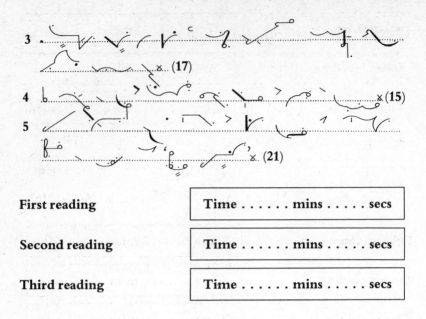

3 .... (17)

4 .... (15)

5 .... (21)

First reading	Time . . . . . . mins . . . . . secs
Second reading	Time . . . . . . mins . . . . . secs
Third reading	Time . . . . . . mins . . . . . secs

UNIT 13 (*Page 59, First Course*)

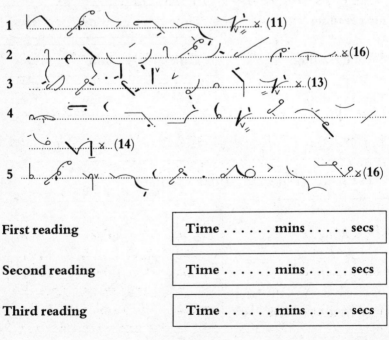

1 .... (11)

2 .... (16)

3 .... (13)

4 ....
.... (14)

5 .... (16)

First reading	Time . . . . . . mins . . . . . secs
Second reading	Time . . . . . . mins . . . . . secs
Third reading	Time . . . . . . mins . . . . . secs

UNIT 13 *(Page 60, First Course)*

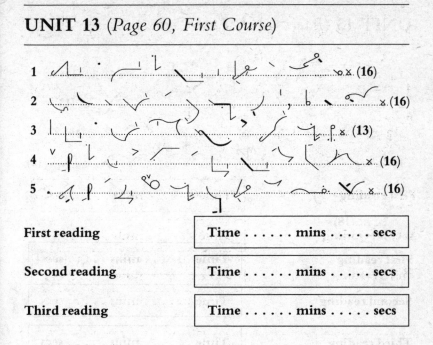

1 .... (16)
2 .... (16)
3 .... (13)
4 .... (16)
5 .... (16)

First reading	Time . . . . . . mins . . . . . secs
Second reading	Time . . . . . . mins . . . . . secs
Third reading	Time . . . . . . mins . . . . . secs

UNIT 13 *(Pages 60–1, First Course)*

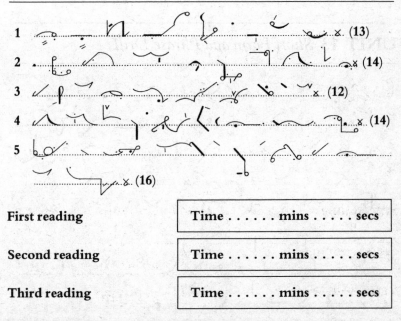

1 .... (13)
2 .... (14)
3 .... (12)
4 .... (14)
5 .... (16)

First reading	Time . . . . . . mins . . . . . secs
Second reading	Time . . . . . . mins . . . . . secs
Third reading	Time . . . . . . mins . . . . . secs

UNIT 13 *(Pages 62–3, First Course)*

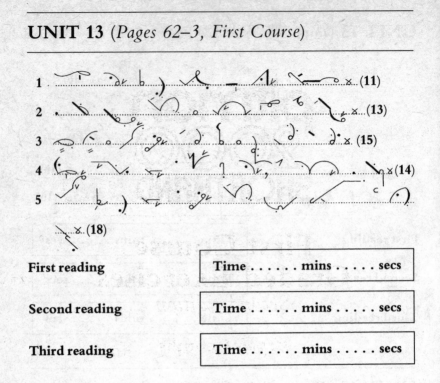

First reading | Time . . . . . . mins . . . . . secs

Second reading | Time . . . . . . mins . . . . . secs

Third reading | Time . . . . . . mins . . . . . secs

UNIT 13 *Short Form and Phrase Drill*

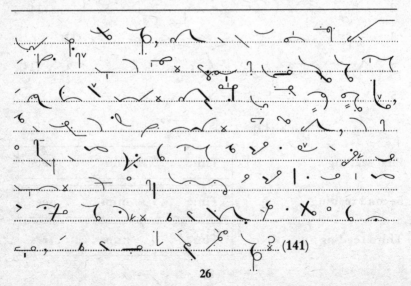

First reading | Time . . . . . mins . . . . . secs

Second reading | Time . . . . . mins . . . . . secs

Third reading | Time . . . . . mins . . . . . secs

UNIT 14 (*Page 66, First Course*)

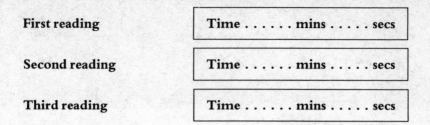

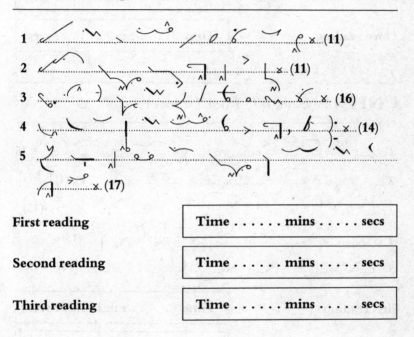

First reading | Time . . . . . . mins . . . . . secs

Second reading | Time . . . . . . mins . . . . . secs

Third reading | Time . . . . . . mins . . . . . secs

UNIT 14 (*Pages 67–9, First Course*)

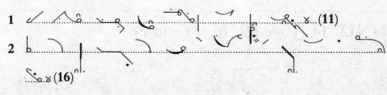

27

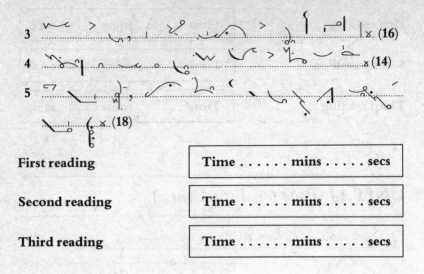

3 .... x (16)

4 .... x (14)

5 ....
.... x (18)

First reading	Time . . . . . mins . . . . . secs
Second reading	Time . . . . . mins . . . . . secs
Third reading	Time . . . . . mins . . . . . secs

UNIT 14 (*Page 69, First Course*)

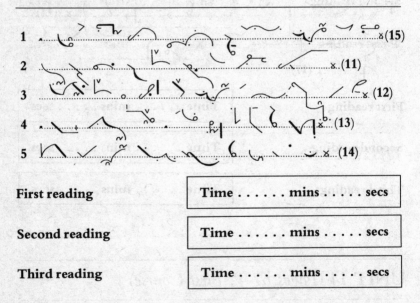

1 .... x (15)

2 .... x (11)

3 .... x (12)

4 .... x (13)

5 .... x (14)

First reading	Time . . . . . mins . . . . . secs
Second reading	Time . . . . . mins . . . . . secs
Third reading	Time . . . . . mins . . . . . secs

UNIT 14 (*Page 69, First Course*)

1 .... x (11)

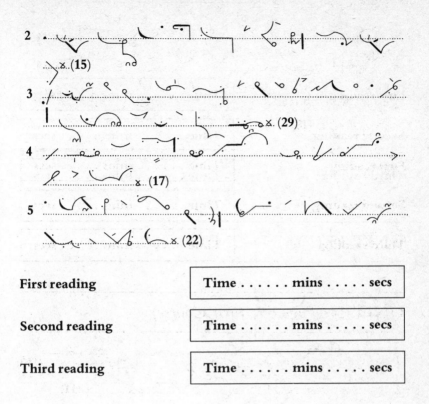

2 ... x. **(15)**

3 ... x. **(29)**

4 ... x. **(17)**

5 ... x. **(22)**

First reading	Time . . . . . mins . . . . . secs
Second reading	Time . . . . . mins . . . . . secs
Third reading	Time . . . . . mins . . . . . secs

UNIT 14 *Short Form and Phrase Drill*

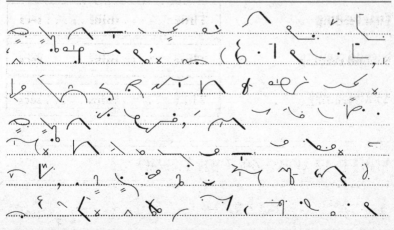

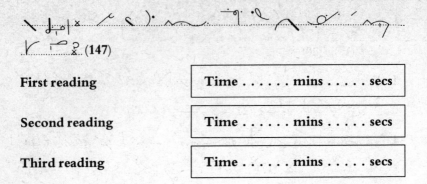

(147)

First reading	Time . . . . . . mins . . . . . secs
Second reading	Time . . . . . . mins . . . . . secs
Third reading	Time . . . . . . mins . . . . . secs

UNIT 15 (Pages 71–2, First Course)

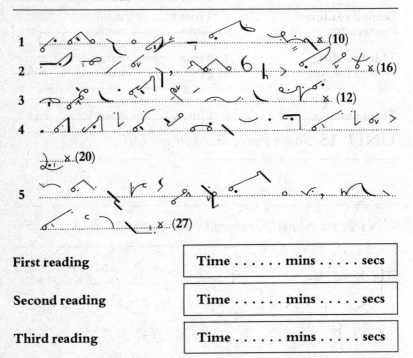

1   (10)
2   (16)
3   (12)
4   (20)
5   (27)

First reading	Time . . . . . . mins . . . . . secs
Second reading	Time . . . . . . mins . . . . . secs
Third reading	Time . . . . . . mins . . . . . secs

UNIT 15 (Page 72, First Course)

1   (17)

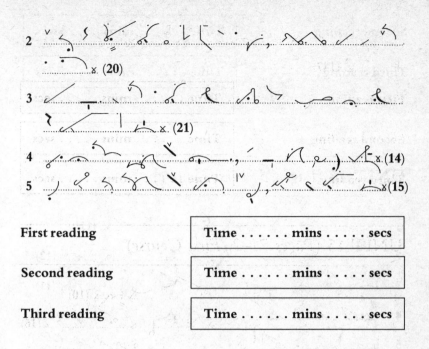

2 .... x. (20)

3 .... x. (21)

4 .... (14)

5 .... (15)

First reading	Time . . . . . mins . . . . . secs
Second reading	Time . . . . . mins . . . . . secs
Third reading	Time . . . . . mins . . . . . secs

UNIT 15 *Short Form and Phrase Drill*

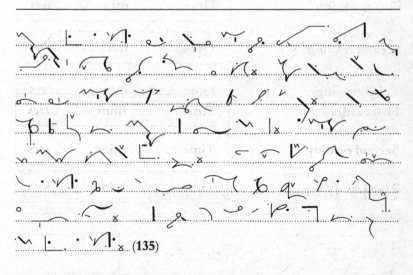

.... x.. (135)

First reading	Time . . . . . mins . . . . . secs

Second reading   Time . . . . . mins . . . . . secs

Third reading   Time . . . . . mins . . . . . secs

UNIT 16 (*Page 75, First Course*)

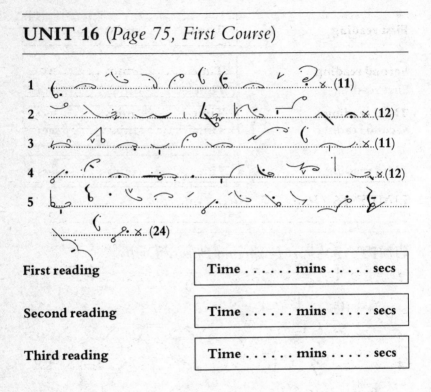

1 .... x (11)
2 .... x (12)
3 .... x (11)
4 .... x (12)
5 .... x (24)

First reading   Time . . . . . mins . . . . . secs

Second reading   Time . . . . . mins . . . . . secs

Third reading   Time . . . . . mins . . . . . secs

UNIT 16 (*Page 76, First Course*)

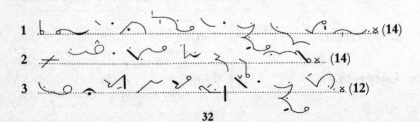

1 .... x (14)
2 .... x (14)
3 .... x (12)

32

4 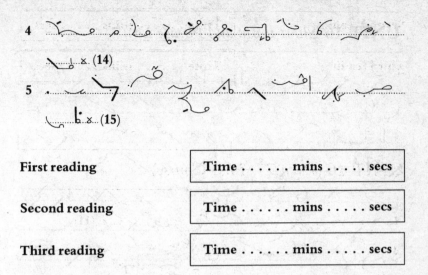 **(14)**

5 **(15)**

First reading	Time . . . . . . mins . . . . . secs
Second reading	Time . . . . . . mins . . . . . secs
Third reading	Time . . . . . . mins . . . . . secs

UNIT 16 (*Page 77, First Course*)

1 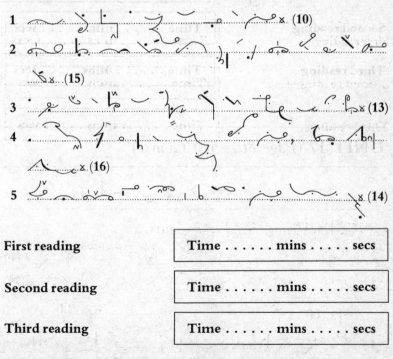 **x. (10)**

2 **x. (15)**

3 **x. (13)**

4 **x. (16)**

5 **x. (14)**

First reading	Time . . . . . . mins . . . . . secs
Second reading	Time . . . . . . mins . . . . . secs
Third reading	Time . . . . . . mins . . . . . secs

UNIT 16 *Short Form and Phrase Drill*

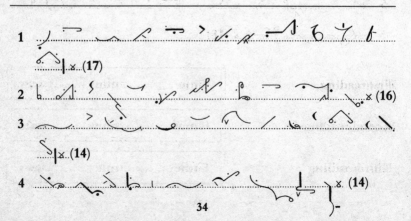

(153)

First reading	Time . . . . . . mins . . . . . secs
Second reading	Time . . . . . . mins . . . . . secs
Third reading	Time . . . . . . mins . . . . . secs

UNIT 17 *(Page 80, First Course)*

1 .... (17)

2 .... (16)

3 ....

.... (14)

4 .... (14)

34

5 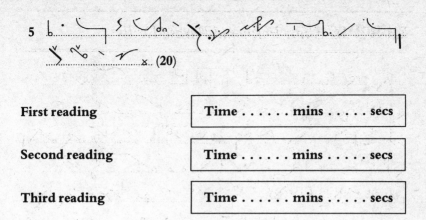 (20)

First reading	Time . . . . . . mins . . . . . secs

Second reading	Time . . . . . . mins . . . . . secs

Third reading	Time . . . . . . mins . . . . . secs

UNIT 17 (Page 81, First Course)

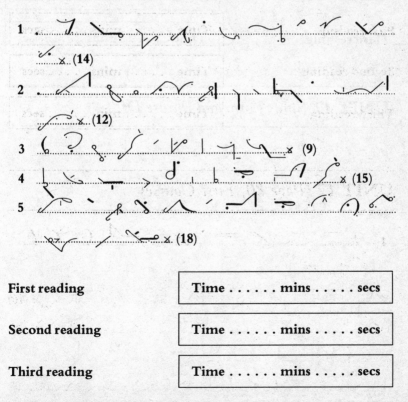

1 .... (14)

2 .... (12)

3 .... (9)

4 .... (15)

5 .... (18)

First reading	Time . . . . . . mins . . . . . secs

Second reading	Time . . . . . . mins . . . . . secs

Third reading	Time . . . . . . mins . . . . . secs

UNIT 17 (*Page 83, First Course*)

1 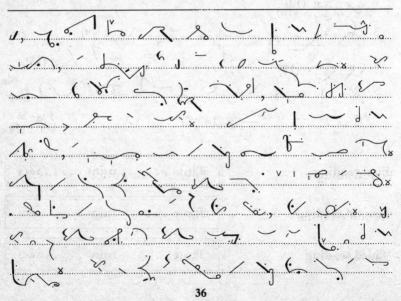 (12)

2 (16)

3 (13)

4 (14)

5 (12)

First reading	Time . . . . . . mins . . . . . secs

Second reading	Time . . . . . . mins . . . . . secs

Third reading	Time . . . . . . mins . . . . . secs

UNIT 17 *Short Form and Phrase Drill*

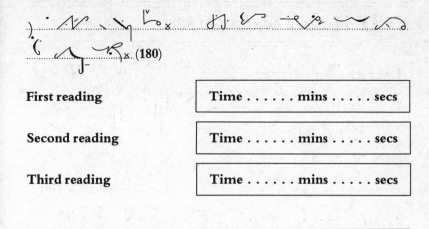

(180)

First reading	Time . . . . . . mins . . . . . secs
Second reading	Time . . . . . . mins . . . . . secs
Third reading	Time . . . . . . mins . . . . . secs

UNIT 18 *(Page 85, First Course)*

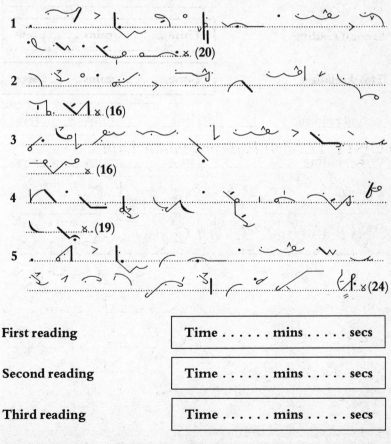

1 .... (20)

2 .... (16)

3 .... (16)

4 .... (19)

5 .... (24)

First reading	Time . . . . . . mins . . . . . secs
Second reading	Time . . . . . . mins . . . . . secs
Third reading	Time . . . . . . mins . . . . . secs

UNIT 18 *(Page 86, First Course)*

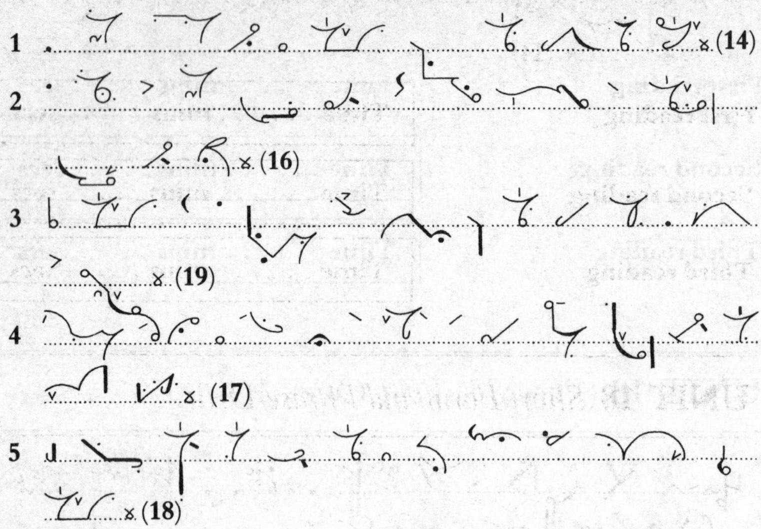

1 *(shorthand)* . (14)

2 *(shorthand)*

(shorthand) . (16)

3 *(shorthand)*

(shorthand) . (19)

4 *(shorthand)*

(shorthand) . (17)

5 *(shorthand)*

(shorthand) . (18)

First reading	Time . . . . . . mins . . . . . secs
Second reading	Time . . . . . . mins . . . . . secs
Third reading	Time . . . . . . mins . . . . . secs

UNIT 18 *(Page 87, First Course)*

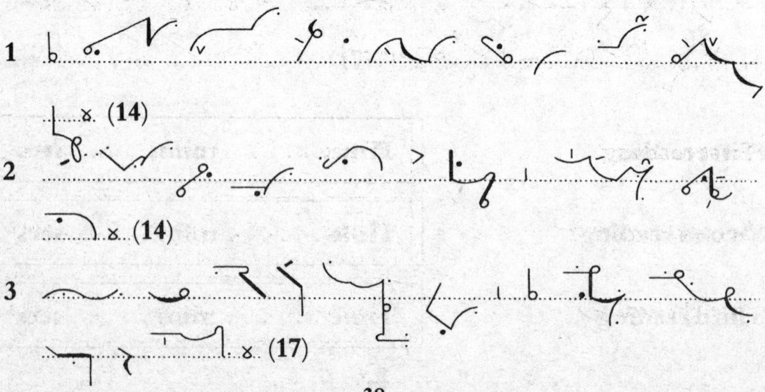

1 *(shorthand)*

(shorthand) . (14)

2 *(shorthand)*

(shorthand) . (14)

3 *(shorthand)*

(shorthand) . (17)

4 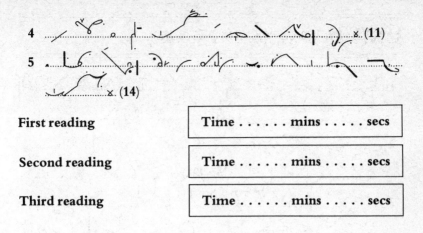 x. (11)

5 x. (14)

First reading	Time . . . . . . mins . . . . . secs
Second reading	Time . . . . . . mins . . . . . secs
Third reading	Time . . . . . . mins . . . . . secs

UNIT 18 *Short Form and Phrase Drill*

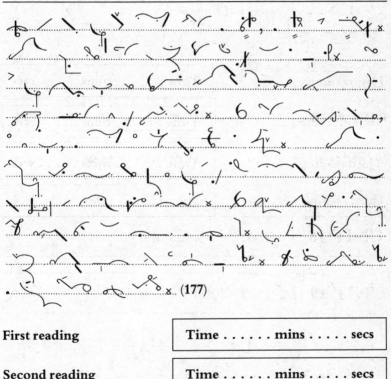

(177)

First reading	Time . . . . . . mins . . . . . secs
Second reading	Time . . . . . . mins . . . . . secs
Third reading	Time . . . . . . mins . . . . . secs

UNIT 19 *(Page 90, First Course)*

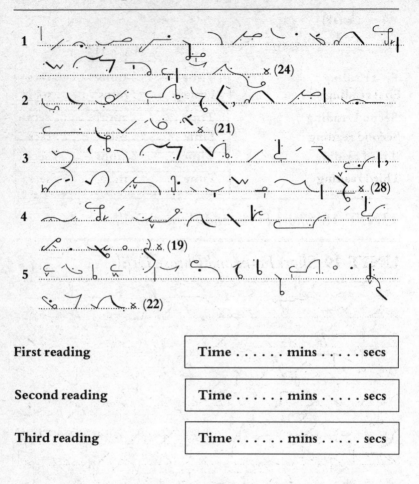

1   .... × (24)

2   .... × (21)

3   .... × (28)

4   .... × (19)

5   .... × (22)

First reading	Time . . . . . . mins . . . . . secs
Second reading	Time . . . . . . mins . . . . . secs
Third reading	Time . . . . . . mins . . . . . secs

UNIT 19 *(Page 91, First Course)*

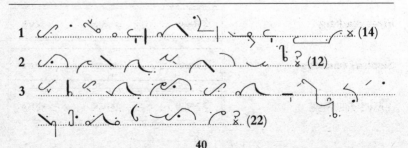

1   .... × (14)

2   .... × (12)

3   .... × (22)

4 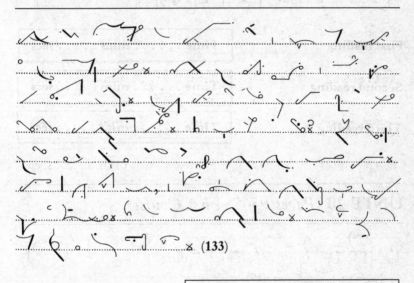 **(19)**

5 .... **(12)**

First reading	Time . . . . . mins . . . . . secs

Second reading	Time . . . . . mins . . . . . secs

Third reading	Time . . . . . mins . . . . . secs

UNIT 19 *Short Form and Phrase Drill*

(133)

First reading	Time . . . . . mins . . . . . secs

Second reading	Time . . . . . mins . . . . . secs

Third reading	Time . . . . . mins . . . . . secs

UNIT 20 *(Pages 94–5, First Course)*

1 .... (shorthand outline) .... x (25)

2 ...... (shorthand outline) .... x (16)

3 ...... (shorthand outline) .... x (20)

4 ...... (shorthand outline) .... x (15)

5 ...... (shorthand outline) .... x (24)

First reading	Time . . . . . . mins . . . . . secs
Second reading	Time . . . . . . mins . . . . . secs
Third reading	Time . . . . . . mins . . . . . secs

UNIT 20 *(Pages 95–7, First Course)*

1 ...... (shorthand outline) .... x (19)

2 ...... (shorthand outline) .... x (20)

3 ...... (shorthand outline) .... x (13)

42

4 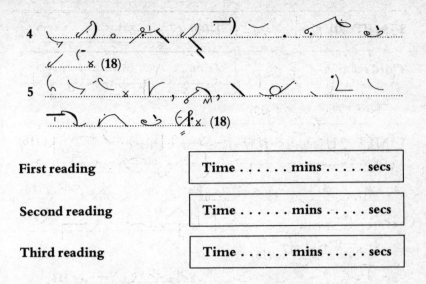 (18)

5 (18)

First reading	Time . . . . . . mins . . . . . secs

Second reading	Time . . . . . . mins . . . . . secs

Third reading	Time . . . . . . mins . . . . . secs

UNIT 20 *Short Form and Phrase Drill*

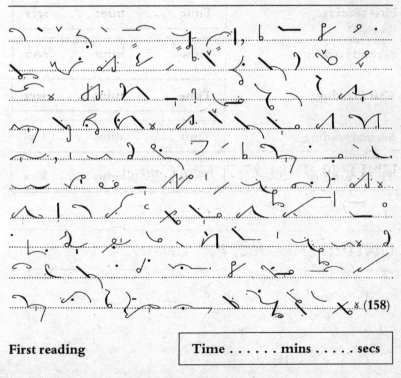

(158)

First reading	Time . . . . . . mins . . . . . secs

43

Second reading Time . . . . . mins . . . . . secs

Third reading Time . . . . . mins . . . . . secs

UNIT 21 (*Pages 100–1, First Course*)

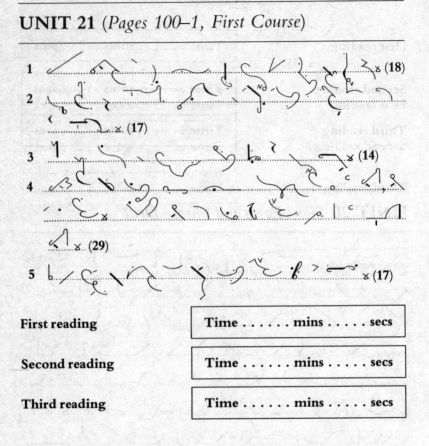

1 ... **(18)**
2 ...
(17)
3 ... **(14)**
4 ...
(29)
5 ... **(17)**

First reading Time . . . . . mins . . . . . secs

Second reading Time . . . . . mins . . . . . secs

Third reading Time . . . . . mins . . . . . secs

UNIT 21 (*Page 102, First Course*)

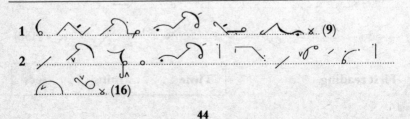

1 ... **(9)**
2 ...
(16)

44

3 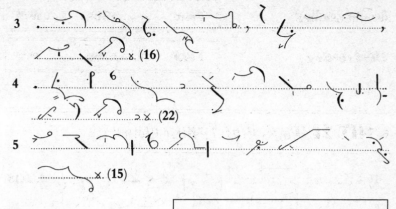 (16)

4 (22)

5 (15)

First reading	Time . . . . . mins . . . . . secs
Second reading	Time . . . . . mins . . . . . secs
Third reading	Time . . . . . mins . . . . . secs

UNIT 21 *Short Form and Phrase Drill*

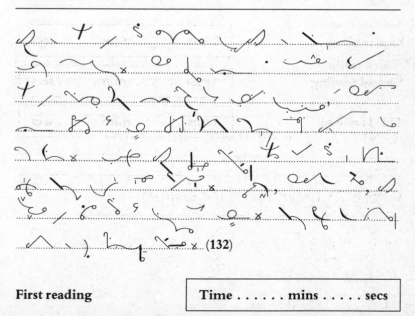 (132)

First reading Time . . . . . mins . . . . . secs

45

Second reading

Time . . . . . mins . . . . . secs

Third reading

Time . . . . . mins . . . . . secs

UNIT 22 *(Page 106, First Course)*

1 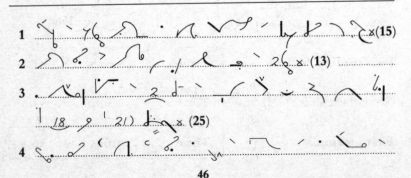 x (14)

2 ... x (16)

3 ... x (12)

4 ... x (18)

5 ... x (14)

First reading

Time . . . . . mins . . . . . secs

Second reading

Time . . . . . mins . . . . . secs

Third reading

Time . . . . . mins . . . . . secs

UNIT 22 *(Pages 107–10, First Course)*

1 ... x (15)

2 ... x (13)

3 ... 18 21) x (25)

4 ...

46

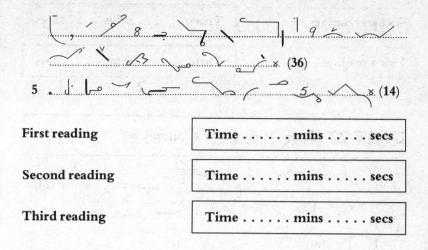

(36)

5 ... **(14)**

First reading	Time . . . . . . mins . . . . . secs

Second reading	Time . . . . . . mins . . . . . secs

Third reading	Time . . . . . . mins . . . . . secs

UNIT 22 *Short Form and Phrase Drill*

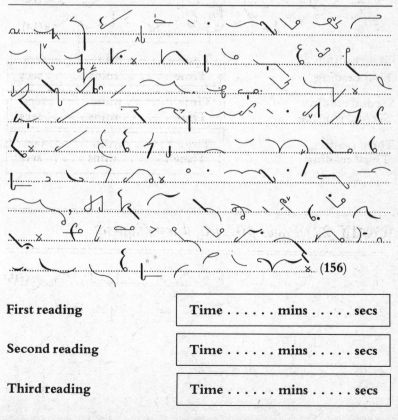

(156)

First reading	Time . . . . . . mins . . . . . secs

Second reading	Time . . . . . . mins . . . . . secs

Third reading	Time . . . . . . mins . . . . . secs

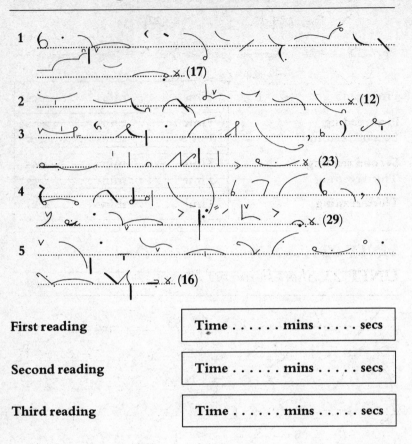

1 ...... (17)

2 ...... x (12)

3 ...... x (23)

4 ...... x (29)

5 ...... x (16)

First reading	Time . . . . . . mins . . . . . secs
Second reading	Time . . . . . . mins . . . . . secs
Third reading	Time . . . . . . mins . . . . . secs

UNIT 23 *(Pages 114–15, First Course)*

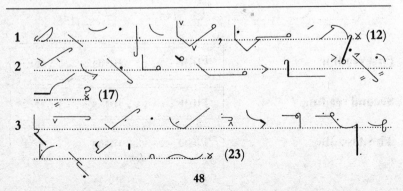

1 ...... x (12)

2 ...... ? (17)

3 ...... x (23)

4 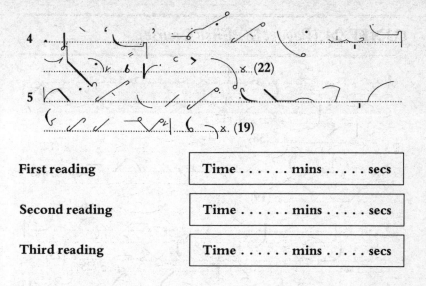 (22)

5 (19)

First reading	Time . . . . . . mins . . . . . secs

Second reading	Time . . . . . . mins . . . . . secs

Third reading	Time . . . . . . mins . . . . . secs

UNIT 23 *Short Form and Phrase Drill*

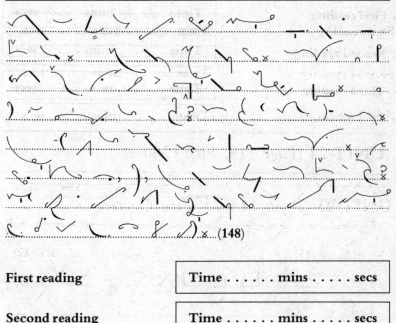 (148)

First reading	Time . . . . . . mins . . . . . secs

Second reading	Time . . . . . . mins . . . . . secs

Third reading	Time . . . . . . mins . . . . . secs

UNIT 24 *(Page 118, First Course)*

1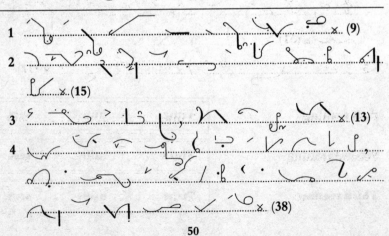

(38)

2 ... **(19)**

3 ... **(23)**

4 ... **(13)**

5 ... **(13)**

First reading	Time . . . . . mins . . . . . secs
Second reading	Time . . . . . mins . . . . . secs
Third reading	Time . . . . . mins . . . . . secs

UNIT 24 *(Page 119, First Course)*

1 ... **(9)**

2 ...

... **(15)**

3 ... **(13)**

4 ...

... **(38)**

50

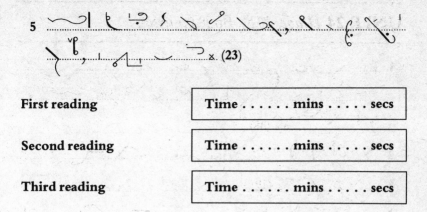

5 .... (23)

First reading	Time . . . . . . mins . . . . . secs

Second reading	Time . . . . . . mins . . . . . secs

Third reading	Time . . . . . . mins . . . . . secs

UNIT 24 (*Page 120, First Course*)

1 .... (22)

2 .... (12)

3 .... (22)

4 .... (31)

5 .... (12)

First reading	Time . . . . . . mins . . . . . secs

Second reading	Time . . . . . . mins . . . . . secs

Third reading	Time . . . . . . mins . . . . . secs

UNIT 24 *(Pages 121–3, First Course)*

1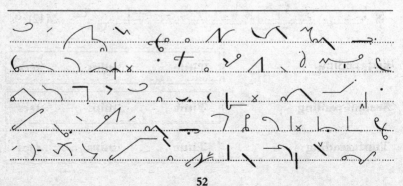

(26)

2 *(18)*

3 *(18)*

4 *(17)*

5 *(13)*

First reading	Time . . . . . . mins . . . . . secs
Second reading	Time . . . . . . mins . . . . . secs
Third reading	Time . . . . . . mins . . . . . secs

UNIT 24 *Short Form and Phrase Drill*

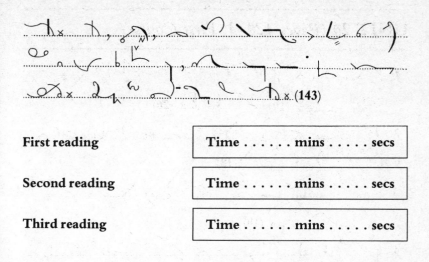

(143)

First reading	Time . . . . . . mins . . . . . secs
Second reading	Time . . . . . . mins . . . . . secs
Third reading	Time . . . . . . mins . . . . . secs

UNIT 25 *(Page 127, First Course)*

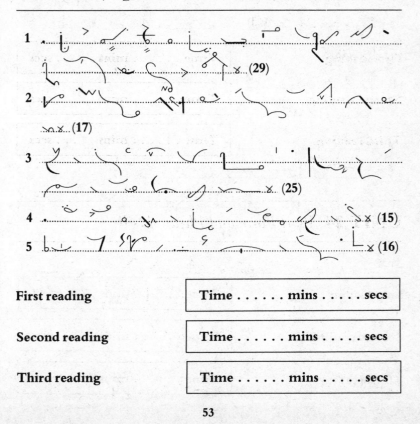

1   (29)

2   (17)

3   (25)

4   (15)

5   (16)

First reading	Time . . . . . . mins . . . . . secs
Second reading	Time . . . . . . mins . . . . . secs
Third reading	Time . . . . . . mins . . . . . secs

UNIT 25 (*Pages 128–9, First Course*)

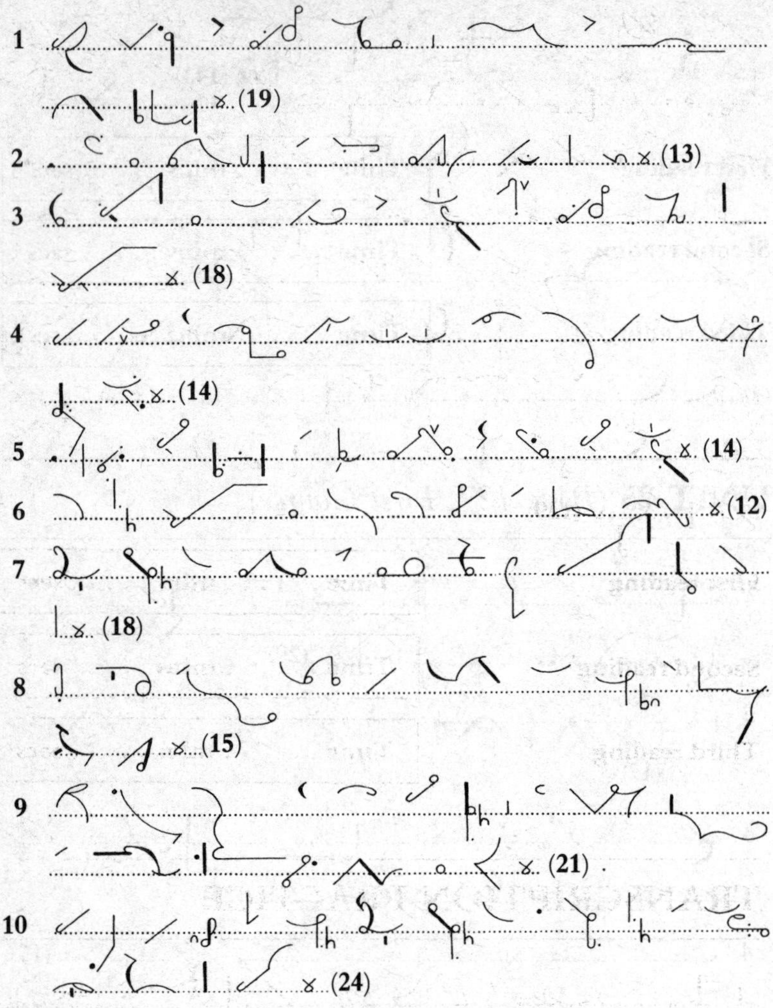

1 (19)

2 (13)

3 (18)

4 (14)

5 (14)

6 (12)

7 (18)

8 (15)

9 (21)

10 (24)

First reading	Time . . . . . . mins . . . . . secs
Second reading	Time . . . . . . mins . . . . . secs
Third reading	Time . . . . . . mins . . . . . secs

UNIT 25 *Short Form and Phrase Drill*

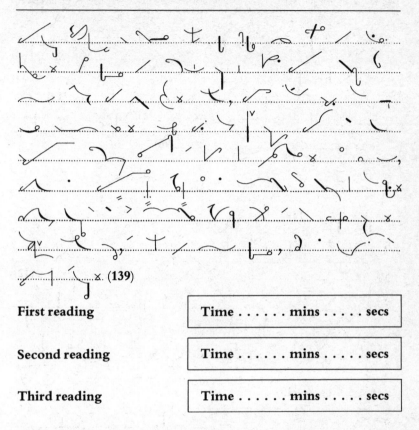

...x. (139)

First reading	Time . . . . . mins . . . . . secs
Second reading	Time . . . . . mins . . . . . secs
Third reading	Time . . . . . mins . . . . . secs

TRANSCRIPTION PRACTICE

1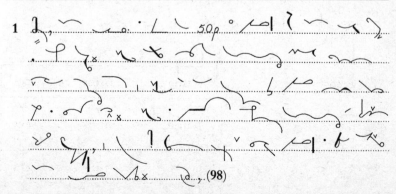

...(98)

2 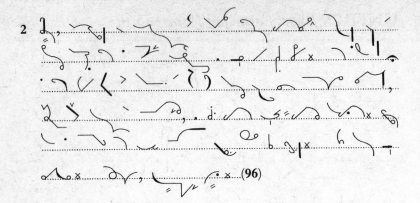 (96)

3 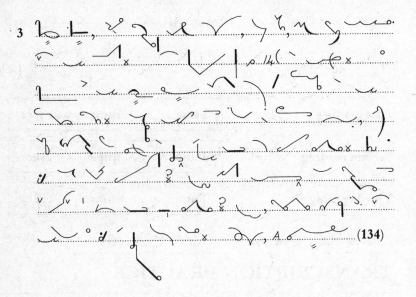 (134)

4 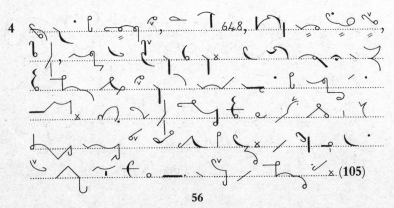 (105)

5 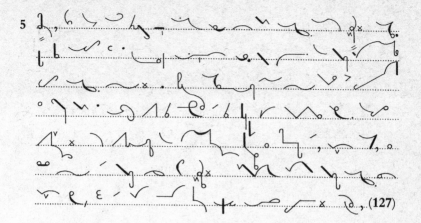 **(127)**

6 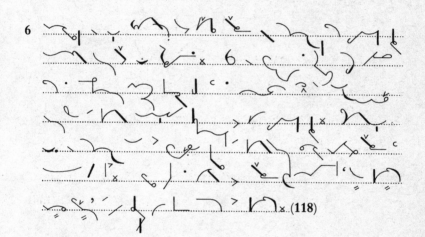 **(118)**

7 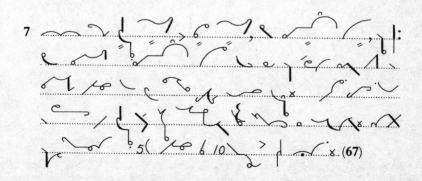 **(67)**

57

UNIT 1 (*Page 4, First Course*)

1 Pay the aid to tow the boat to his space. (**10**)
2 It is his day to stay and pose. (**8**)
3 Pay the aid to date the tape today. (**8**)
4 Tape the date to the base of his boat. (**9**)
5 Today is the day to stow the spades and bait. (**10**)
6 Is it his oboe? (**4**)
7 Space the tape and date it today. (**7**)
8 The pay is to aid his boats. (**7**)
9 His aid is to stay today to stow the oats. (**10**)
10 Is it his soap? (**4**)

UNIT 1 *Short Form and Phrase Drill*

1 Tow it to his space. (**5**)
2 The boat is to tow it. (**6**)
3 Tape it to the base of the boat. (**8**)
4 Pay the aid today. (**4**)
5 Is today's date to stay? (**5**)
6 It is his boat and his spade. (**7**)
7 It is his oboe. (**4**)
8 It is the day and the date. (**7**)
9 The pay is to aid his stay. (**7**)
10 Is it the date of the tape? (**7**)

UNIT 2 (*Page 6, First Course*)

1 It is his aim to own his boat. (**8**)
2 Tow the oak boat and go to the bay. (**9**)
3 Tape his toe and the ache may go. (**8**)
4 No, today is the day to pay his aid. (**9**)
5 His aim is to go to tape his own boat. (**10**)

UNIT 2 (*Page 6, First Course*)

1 I do know the names of the boats and I know the boating game.
(**14**)
2 It is going to take days to make the cakes and I may go to his aid.
(**17**)

3 It is his aim to make his own boats of oak. (**11**)
4 You may take anything to the boat in the bay and stay and do nothing. (**15**)
5 It is going to pay you to stay to make something to take to his aid. (**16**)

UNIT 2 *Short Form and Phrase Drill*

I know the boat is to go in his name / and it is to stay in the bay. Do you / know anything of the aim of his taking it? You / may know something of the date it is to go. / Is it today you do something to tape the boat? / I know nothing of the two tapes. I do go / boating in any of the bays and I know something / of coping in boats. You and I may go in / his boat to take the things to the bay. Take / his space in the boat and you may stay the / day. It pays to know something of boating today. (**109**)

UNIT 3 *(Page 9, First Course)*

---

1 The cases of both of the folk stay in the same bay. (**12**)
2 They may vote to save, and make safe, both of the bases. (**12**)
3 The faith of the folk in the boat may fade and go. (**12**)
4 They both know it is safe to bathe in the bay. (**11**)
5 Mauve is in vogue, though they both know of cases of fading. (**12**)

UNIT 3 *(Page 9, First Course)*

---

1 You may pay the same and take both cases. (**9**)
2 It makes sense to pay debts and to save. (**9**)
3 Both of them may take the oath though the case is vague. (**12**)
4 It makes no sense to guess the name of the make of the boat. (**14**)
5 Take the cases of eggs to the deck and save space. (**11**)

UNIT 3 *(Page 11, First Course)*

---

1 Something may come to some of the folk in a month. (**11**)
2 In the month of May I stay in the setting sun up to dusk. (**14**)
3 It is his custom to take his son to a pub in Exmouth. (**13**)

4 Do you know it is unsafe to doze in the sun? (**11**)
5 Kay may take a tub of gum to tape the base of the boat. (**14**)

UNIT 3 *Short Form and Phrase Drill*

It takes months to save enough to get the aid / to all the folk. Thank you for anything you may / be doing for them. I know it is the custom / to aid all of them and I thank the folk / in the pub for the sums they save in the / keg to aid all the folk. With all the sums / coming in this month, and in May, I know it / is safe to aid all of them. (**77**)

UNIT 4 (*Page 13, First Course*)

1 The boat is setting sail with the load of soap to sell in Low Lake.
(**15**)
2 The loading and selling of spades is slow and they have low sales.
(**13**)
3 Lessons in sailing develop the lungs and the muscles of the legs.
(**12**)
4 With the delays in loading the cases of eggs you may have less to sell. (**15**)
5 You may pay less for the lengths of sail they sell. (**11**)

UNIT 4 (*Page 15, First Course*)

1 Weigh the load and take it to the yellow boat. (**10**)
2 The way they loaded the coal may well have delayed the Wednesday sailing. (**13**)
3 The swaying of the boat in the lake swell dazed the young folk.
(**13**)
4 Yes, they may well be faced with all the unpaid debts. (**11**)
5 The wedding is delayed and the young folk may have to stay for the day. (**15**)

UNIT 4 *Short Form and Phrase Drill*

You will be thanked for aiding them in the boat / yesterday. They will do less sailing in the yellow boat / and they will have to take lessons. It will be / up to you to develop lessons for them. They will / do anything you set them to do. You may have / to go to the lake for months but you will / be paid. I know you will do well but you / will have to wake them up. They have to sail / boats and we have to make sailing safe. They will / have faith in you and it will be nothing but / a lesson for them and for you. They will be / slow, as is the case with some of the young, / but you will have something to aim for and they / will make a name for themselves. (**136**)

UNIT 5 (*Page 18, First Course*)

1 May will pay for a dozen red and yellow roses. (**10**)
2 The purpose of the rungs of rope is to get the folk to the deck but they swayed as the red boat rose and they fell in the swell. (**29**)
3 It may be as slow to go to the road as it is to go to the railway. (**18**)
4 The girls worked well and they sold dozens of red roses and yellow birds. (**14**)
5 The girl boarded the bus to go to work. (**9**)
6 The young birds pecked the cake in the furrow. (**9**)
7 The work Ray does in boarding up the burrow is thorough. (**11**)
8 Work with a will and a purpose and be thorough in all you do. (**14**)
9 They roped the wreck to a board and towed it the length of the road to the railway. (**18**)
10 I have no faith in the Railway Board but they will be thanked for the work they do. (**18**)

UNIT 5 (*Page 19, First Course*)

1 Repair the door for the customer and make it the same colour as the gate. (**15**)
2 The oars were old and we were forced to repair them. (**11**)
3 We have to care for the earth and all its rare resources. (**12**)
4 The nurses were caring for the girls in the firm. (**10**)
5 A term with the firm in Rome is fair for some but unfair for you. (**15**)

UNIT 5 *Short Form and Phrase Drill*

Will your firm manufacture all our cases for us? Thank / you for manufacturing some of the cases in all the / colours yesterday. It will be up to us to get / them to our customers today, and our firm will pay / the road and railway fares for our girls to take / them to Exmouth and Dunmow. As you will be the / sole manufacturer of the cases we are going to sell / yours to our customers in Rome too. With you as / our manufacturers I know we will have no delays and / this aids our firm and our customers. (**97**)

UNIT 6 (*Page 23, First Course*)

1 The pets came to the port late in the day but the vet met them. (**15**)
2 The cut in the weight of the coats you manufacture for us is noted. (**14**)
3 We left the late bedding roses for you to cut, but they are dead. (**14**)
4 I left you a note late yesterday, and yet you kept Kate waiting. (**13**)
5 A note is kept of the weight of the babes and it is left for the nurses. (**17**)

UNIT 6 (*Pages 24–5, First Course*)

1 As I expected your methods of exporting do work and they will get results. (**14**)
2 The results of the report are as we expected and the cuts are suffocating exports. (**15**)
3 The experts are expected to debate for some months the effects of the cuts in resources for railroads and subways. (**20**)
4 We wrote to tell them we may deduct the sum to pay the rates. (**14**)

UNIT 6 *Short Form and Phrase Drill*

I think it is up to the manufacturer to let / you know that the ropes and buckets will be late. / We were going to take all the manufactures but this / delay could result in less exports. I know you wrote / to them but you will have to wait days for / any results and the customers will be faced with delays. / I know they were supposed to come this month and / that today is the expected date. Is it too late / to expect anything to come today? We were making reports / yesterday and I think it may well be a case / of waiting, and we may have to make it up / to our customers in some way. Do you know of / anything we could do to save face? (**127**)

UNIT 7 *(Page 28, First Course)*

1 You will have to check the rates of exchange to make your budget work. **(14)**
2 Much of the checking of the pages will result in changes. **(11)**
3 You will be the judge, and it will be up to you to check all the pages. **(17)**
4 The ageing Judge Page came in a jumbo jet. **(9)**
5 His cases were checked and the weights were the same as the budget. **(13)**

UNIT 7 *(Pages 28–30, First Course)*

1 The show is such a change that folk are rushing to go to it. **(14)**
2 The oak is cut and shaved to the shape of the shell of the boat. **(15)**
3 They all say the escapes were so slow, but they were daring. **(12)**
4 We shall rush the work and it will take us four hours to do the sewing. **(16)**
5 The judges said that the estate roses were of such perfect shape, colour and shade that they will sell well. **(20)**

UNIT 7 *Short Form and Phrase Drill*

Will you come with us to our estate to check / the roses which will be on show on Monday? Which / of the shows will you go to? We are thinking / of going to all of them. We shall expect you / to come with us and in that way we shall / all save on the fares. I have had a note / to say that the railways will be having delays on / some days so it will be as well to go / in a coach. We shall be on the road for / hours but we shall have lunch on the way. It / will make a change for you and for us so / do say you will come. I will let you know / of any change in date. We shall be expecting a / note to tell us that you will be coming with / us. **(141)**

UNIT 8 *(Page 32, First Course)*

1 Some of the days are dark in March and the farmer has to rush his work. **(16)**
2 You may park the car in any part of the market in March. **(13)**
3 The guards may have to take arms and march to Archway Road today. **(13)**

4 It is too far to go and we shall have to take the car for part of the way. (**19**)

5 They regard the pass mark as being far too low. (**10**)

UNIT 8 *(Page 33, First Course)*

1 On Saturday we wrote away for a door catch and we sent them cash. (**14**)

2 The fact is you may cash cheques at some banks on Saturdays. (**12**)

3 You will have to adapt your ways to the banking hours and bank your cash on Mondays. (**17**)

4 Some months ago we adapted our cars at the bank so that our guards could act in the case of any attack to take the cash. (**26**)

5 It is a bad Act and we shall attack it at the debate on Saturday. (**15**)

UNIT 8 *(Page 34, First Course)*

1 The lawyer talked for too long and his jaws ached. (**10**)

2 The tall girl and the smaller girl walk to work. (**10**)

3 They thought a talk on the law would make sense. (**10**)

4 We thought the small case we bought you would be large enough. (**12**)

5 I saw the lawyers walking away but I caught up with them and had a talk. (**16**)

UNIT 8 *(Pages 34–5, First Course)*

1 The shop was selling lots of watches at a loss. (**10**)

2 The docks are not a long way off and we shall go for a job. (**15**)

3 The job in the shop was the wrong job for Tom. (**11**)

4 They were opposed to the song because it was not at the top of the charts, but it was selling well. (**21**)

5 'Top' soap will wash off any mark and was developed for all washing jobs. (**14**)

UNIT 8 *Short Form and Phrase Drill*

They always owe us something and they say they will / pay tomorrow. Although our charges are low they have owed / a large sum for months. We shall have to say / to them that they will have to pay off the / balance tomorrow or we shall go to law and they / will also have to pay the lawyer's charges. I think / it will be up to us to do something to / change our charges. We ought to act today to cut / any losses. It would be a case of raising our / charges on selected things we manufacture, owing to the slow / way our markets have developed and also to the large / debts we are owed. It is not of our doing / but we are left with the bad results. We always / ought to think of tomorrow. (**135**)

UNIT 9 (*Pages 38–40, First Course*)

1 The local places all close today and the bank clerks have no work. (**13**)
2 It is pleasant to take the cable car which is close to the motel at which we are staying. (**19**)
3 The clutch plate of the car was blocked and the repair place was closed. (**14**)
4 I have samples of the local glassware which has a black glaze. (**12**)
5 The label on the blanket claims that it is a local cloth. (**12**)

UNIT 9 (*Page 40, First Course*)

1 The attaché case has replaced the satchel in the class today. (**11**)
2 We shall explore his claim and enclose a report on the cattle. (**12**)
3 'We always have a battle with a glut or a shortage!' exclaimed the farmer. (**14**)
4 We are exploring making petals with all the oak cuttings and shavings. (**12**)
5 The bottle exploded splashing the metal model and the results were fatal. (**12**)

UNIT 9 *Short Form and Phrase Drill*

Largely because of the low manufacturing charges, we are able / to sell in such a large way. Who will be / able to cut our manufacturers' rates? I think it would / be fair to say that I know of no local / manufacturer who is able to make things at anything close / to our charges. Our customers are able to afford to / sample anything manufactured today, and this also adds to our / sales. Owing to the changing markets, we are not always / able to let you know the rates but we do / expect that today's rates will largely stay the same. Large / savings are always passed on to our customers and we / think that this is the way to make our name / famous. Tomorrow we may be able to think of 'cuts / for cash'. (132)

UNIT 10 (*Page 43, First Course*)

1 I buy and supply a wide range of fires and lights. (11)
2 I would be delighted to apply for the job because I desire a change. (14)
3 It is a nice time for walks in the long daylight hours. (12)
4 I would like to go and explore miles by car. (10)
5 'My Life as a Guide' might be something I would like to buy. (13)

UNIT 10 (*Pages 43–4, First Course*)

1 I may write all the exercises on the page. (9)
2 I expect that some of the items in the table you are typing will be close to the edge of the page. (22)
3 I was exhausted on Monday because I had walked too far. (11)
4 I came to the Ice Show on Wednesday night. (9)
5 I shall exercise my rights and deny this charge. (9)

UNIT 10 (*Pages 44–5, First Course*)

1 I am employed on the oil well, and I am enjoying it. (12)
2 The voice exercises were unavoidable but they were enjoyable. (9)
3 I expect to have a choice in the type of oil for the car. (14)
4 They will rejoice to have such voices in the royal show. (11)
5 Some damage by employees is unavoidable but science today has developed a wide choice of packing to cut losses. (19)

UNIT 10 *Short Form and Phrase Drill*

Without any influence we should be able to think of / tomorrow and although this does not always apply it is / a desirable thing to do. It

should not be left / too late because life is all too short and you / will
have to make choices today which will affect tomorrow's / success. We
shall have to take charge of those things / which influence affairs and
always be on our guard. It / would be something of a shame to have to
make / changes to our lives largely because we were unable to / accept
advice. We owe it to ourselves to think of / tomorrow today. We
should also be thinking of those who / will be asking for our aid. (**116**)

UNIT 11 (*Page 47, First Course*)

1 Several stores have started to cut waste by checking stock and
  costs. (**12**)
2 I suggest that we take most of the guests to the local show at two
  o'clock. (**16**)
3 At last most burst tyres are being tested and I suggest this will cut
  waste and stop lives being lost. (**20**)
4 Most jacket styles start on the west coast and, at last, those for the
  smaller waist will be available next in the stores. (**23**)
5 The results of the last tests will be in the next post and you must
  not waste time opposing them. (**20**)

UNIT 11 (*Page 48, First Course*)

1 A cluster of boys was standing in the mud at the Leicester match.
  (**13**)
2 Posters do get the message to customers much faster and we shall
  send some to Chester. (**16**)
3 Master the forms for the words and you will be able to write faster
  and raise the standard of your notes. (**21**)
4 The words 'sir' and 'madam' should not occur in tomorrow's test
  but I suggest that you master the art of writing the forms for them.
  (**25**)
5 The masters who set the end of term tests are suggesting some
  ways in which we might raise the standard of work. (**22**)

UNIT 11 *Short Form and Phrase Drill*

For the first time we had almost the best results / and this was largely
because of the first-class work / of all of you. We are unable to say
anything / on the way in which the results were sent to / you but we
will be checking up immediately. At first / it was thought this was

influenced by fire in a / posting box but in any case you should not be / too upset with this delay. Almost all of you will / be able to take immediate steps to apply for posts / and several of those who failed this first time will / have lessons to enable them to have tests at the / start of the next term. (**115**)

UNIT 12 (*Page 52, First Course*)

1 I remember preparing a paper entitled 'Spiders, Ants and Wasps' and presenting it to the class on a cold day in November. (**22**)
2 The number of dockers will fall in October and December. (**10**)
3 The banker said that supplies of ledger paper were low. (**10**)
4 The paper maker told the Water Board it was not the first time that water was in short supply. (**19**)
5 The dockers had a major voice in labour affairs. (**9**)

UNIT 12 (*Pages 54–5, First Course*)

1 Is it correct to say that the Major will be describing the soccer match to our branch in November? (**19**)
2 The strength of the labour force may be cut back which will demonstrate the effects of the strike. (**18**)
3 A separate recording was made of the banker's amazing talk at the supper. (**13**)
4 We shall go to the Soccer Club's Cider Supper described in the paper. (**13**)
5 It was the express desire of the nursing staff that the stoker should be prescribed some extra tablets for his asthma. (**21**)

UNIT 12 *Short Form and Phrase Drill*

Dear Sir, According to our trade records, your company at / present owes this company a large sum, particulars of which / I am enclosing. The sum owed may, in effect, be / larger but we have not yet totalled the items for / December. I regret to tell you that this company is / unable to act as a banker for your company and / you must take immediate steps to pay off all your / debts. We are expecting you to send us a cheque / some time this month, and this should be for most / of the sum you owe us. We were prepared to / aid you for a short time, but we must have / all that is owing to us paid by May. Yours / faithfully, (**121**)

UNIT 13 (*Page 57, First Course*)

1 We believe you will agree to keep to the deal. (**10**)
2 Leave the team as it is and you will see that they will succeed. (**14**)
3 Please keep clear of the tree as I fear it is going to fall. (**14**)
4 She eats several meals each day and she always has a tea and supper. (**14**)
5 A team of people will teach at the college and I believe they will succeed. (**15**)

UNIT 13 (*Page 58, First Course*)

1 If you wish to visit your sister tomorrow you will be able to make a simple apology for not going last week. (**22**)
2 It will be necessary to build as simply as possible because of the limited sum of money available. (**18**)
3 The Factory Bill will deal with injuries to workers in industry and bring relief to many people. (**17**)
4 It is impossible to visit all the families simply because of the limits of finance. (**15**)
5 We are lucky to have a copy of the daily figures and the monthly statistics to insert in the 'Citizens' Weekly'. (**21**)

UNIT 13 (*Page 59, First Course*)

1 It will be useless for the group to move in July. (**11**)
2 The truth is that both the food and shoe trade results show we are losing money. (**16**)
3 We shall use a blue dye on the shoes you bought in July. (**13**)
4 You must agree that keeping cool this July was impossible in our office buildings. (**14**)
5 It is useless to try to move without using the services of the firm of experts. (**16**)

UNIT 13 (*Page 60, First Course*)

1 We took a look at the book but it was not of any use to us. (**16**)
2 If you have to pull and push to get the shoe on, it is too small. (**16**)
3 It took a full month to bring all the wool into the city. (**13**)

4 I stood at the foot of the rack and took the book off the top shelf. **(16)**

5 The youth stood and shook the spices into the food which was in the mixing bowl. **(16)**

UNIT 13 (*Pages 60-1, First Course*)

1 Miss Kay told the girls that it was a good song to sing. **(13)**
2 The citizens were in no mood to discuss the extra levy at the meeting. **(14)**
3 We stood in the mist near the military missile base all night. **(12)**
4 We have enough time to do a useful job without making too many mistakes. **(14)**
5 It is necessary to increase the number of boots and slippers we make in the factory. **(16)**

UNIT 13 (*Pages 62-3, First Course*)

1 In most areas it is easy to receive good radio programmes. **(11)**
2 The best business policy is to lower the costs and that is obvious. **(13)**
3 Mr Lowe is really serious and says that it is his system to assess all essays. **(16)**
4 They must cooperate to create an ideal trading area, and the earlier the better. **(14)**
5 I realise it is not easy to create a serious policy if you are working with lazy people. **(18)**

UNIT 13 *Short Form and Phrase Drill*

If you are to stay in business in this city, / you will have to put in some extra work and / at least try to cut your costs. Please let us / know trading figures for your business for this month and / let us have them by tomorrow. You will be able / to succeed if you will accept Mrs Smith's advice, and / that is to inspect your staff list immediately. According to / the particulars we have, your trade has dropped to almost / zero this month and that is always a sign of / serious things to come. Your company has traded for many / years and has always had an influence on almost all / the major companies in this area. Who is able to / believe that such a large business as this may close, / and who is able to guess at the possible results / for this city? **(143)**

UNIT 14 (*Page 66, First Course*)

1 We are about to announce our first sale in the south. (**11**)
2 We were powerless to keep the crowd out of the tower. (**11**)
3 Please allow us to tell you about the shower which this company is proud to sell. (**16**)
4 If you have any doubts about announcing this to the crowd, just say so. (**14**)
5 I shall have to go out since I am powerless to do anything about that loud noise. (**17**)

UNIT 14 (*Pages 67–9, First Course*)

1 We refuse to accept the views expressed in the Tuesday newspaper. (**11**)
2 It is your duty to keep your things of value and beauty in a secure place. (**16**)
3 I knew of the feud, but I was unaware of the issues that had caused it. (**16**)
4 I presumed you knew his views about the value of the items in stock. (**14**)
5 According to the book society, we may assume that too few people read newspapers and books these days. (**18**)

UNIT 14 (*Page 69, First Course*)

1 The views of the graduate were similar to those of many individuals in the class. (**15**)
2 Fewer people seem to have time to spare for rescue work. (**11**)
3 Valuable time is wasted by the individual and many opportunities are lost. (**12**)
4 The book reviewer occupies the office situated at the top of this building. (**13**)
5 It will be to our mutual benefit to bring this feud to an end. (**14**)

UNIT 14 (*Page 69, First Course*)

1 The lecture was for the graduate class but few members arrived.
(**11**)
2 The football fixtures have a great effect on the shops situated near the football pitch. (**15**)

3 Each individual has to speak for some minutes on the subject of his choice and we have as a result had fewer failures in the end of term exams. (**29**)

4 Our cousins in Canada send us regular news which we circulate to the rest of the family. (**17**)

5 A valuable set of stamps is to be issued this week and it will be to our mutual benefit to purchase them. (**22**)

UNIT 14 *Short Form and Phrase Drill*

Mr Peters will be going to New York soon and / will be speaking on the topic 'How to succeed in / all subjects'. You may think that this is an odd / subject for a talk, but it was popular here last / year and we know it will be just as successful / in New York. Mr Peters will be away for several / weeks and will not be in the office for at / least a month. It will be up to us to / keep things going in his absence. According to my diary, / the Trade Fair starts towards the end of the month / and I trust that you will be able to assist / me with that particular job. How this business will manage / without extra staff is a subject to be discussed. Are / you able to say how many extra staff will be / necessary and how much it will cost? (**147**)

UNIT 15 *(Pages 71–2, First Course)*

1 He hopes to have his usual good harvest in September. (**10**)

2 Garage costs are high today, and perhaps this is due to the harsh rise in charges. (**16**)

3 Most households have a hot water supply and many have central heating. (**12**)

4 The head waiter at the hotel always seems to be in a great hurry at the height of the season. (**20**)

5 I am happy to be able to tell you that the house beside the harbour is to let, but you will have to hurry with your booking. (**27**)

UNIT 15 *(Page 72, First Course)*

1 Eat wholesome food at home and on holiday, and you should be healthy for the whole year. (**17**)

2 I hear that the Sahara Hotel is at the top of a hill, and perhaps we should hire a car. (**20**)

3 We are going to hire a hotel and several waiters for the next meeting and save all that work at home. **(21)**
4 He may harm himself by smoking, and good health is not easy to restore. **(14)**
5 She was hurting herself by wearing tight shoes, and was not able to walk home. **(15)**

UNIT 15 *Short Form and Phrase Drill*

I hope that he will be able to take a / holiday soon because I know he is working hard and / if he carries on like this he will harm his / health. I think he will benefit by having some sun / and I know that he will enjoy himself just resting / on the beach. Being in business in this city does / tire him and I hope that he will do something / about it. I know that he will listen to you / and I hope you will help by talking to him. / According to my diary he will have some time for / a holiday towards the end of next month and this / is the first time such an opportunity has come along. / Do use your influence and at least get him to / think about taking a holiday. **(135)**

UNIT 16 *(Page 75, First Course)*

1 These men often earn less than those men on the machines. **(11)**
2 In his opinion nothing but genuine business telephone calls should be made. **(12)**
3 Human rights mean no less to men and women than money. **(11)**
4 He alone may examine the coal veins in the mine at noon. **(12)**
5 It is known that he is a fine man and he often pays for the meals of those who are poorer than he is. **(24)**

UNIT 16 *(Page 76, First Course)*

1 It is something of a rare occurrence for an insurance firm to lose money. **(14)**
2 Our company announces a balance at the end of the year to its members. **(14)**
3 Fences made of wood are not always protected by an insurance policy. **(12)**

4 Romance is the essence of these stories whose creators often sell millions of books. (**14**)
5 The new baggage allowances and insurance rates should be announced within the next few days. (**15**)

UNIT 16 (*Page 77, First Course*)

1 Many patients take out an insurance in case of illness. (**10**)
2 Summonses demanding immediate payment were issued and each summons was sent by first-class post. (**15**)
3 A recent find of diamonds in Australia brought about extensive new land settlement. (**13**)
4 The manpower shortage is due to inefficiency as well as illness, and this means reduced revenue. (**16**)
5 Shyness may sometimes cause amusement but it is almost an illness for many people. (**14**)

UNIT 16 *Short Form and Phrase Drill*

A businessman has to be efficient if he is to / succeed, but it will not take him long to realise / that even this is not sufficient. He must have good / men and women working with him and it is the / strength of his manpower which will produce first-class results. / I am sure you will not be surprised to be / told that many a businessman has failed because his work / force was not a team and in any business this / is absolutely vital. According to a recent report it will / not be possible for a businessman to survive for long / without union support. A firm has to make arrangements so / that management and workers do form a team, and this / arrangement has to be successful. We hope to have a / local businessman come along to talk to us about this / subject soon, and we will arrange for all of our / staff to be present. (**154**)

UNIT 17 (*Page 80, First Course*)

1 She can now run again all the way round the garden and this has only just happened. (**17**)
2 It is certain that the people in the eastern and western settlements can maintain the peace. (**16**)

3 Many of the funny things in life are events that happen without being planned. (**14**)
4 Payments should be made upon demand but many modern firms decline to do so. (**14**)
5 It is a fact that the fortunes of both eastern and western countries are affected by the price of oil. (**20**)

UNIT 17 (*Page 81, First Course*)

1 The engine begins to turn within a few minutes as the oil burns away. (**14**)
2 The word spinster is rarely used today to describe an unmarried woman. (**12**)
3 This machine spins wool and turns it into fabric. (**9**)
4 It would be fun to go to the dances but it is against college rules.
(**15**)
5 We must all use the brains we have and guard against allowing lazy habits to spoil our progress. (**18**)

UNIT 17 (*Page 83, First Course*)

1 Students who attend the college may collect grants at the accounts office. (**12**)
2 It is important to attend all shorthand classes to avoid being disappointed with the speed results. (**16**)
3 Indoor tennis is now available so rainy days and darkness are not important. (**13**)
4 The accountant has spoken to the landlord about the rent and the faulty furnace. (**14**)
5 Usually you can depend on someone for help to a certain extent.
(**12**)

UNIT 17 *Short Form and Phrase Drill*

Gentlemen, in these hard times we cannot be responsible for / any debts about which the accountant is unaware, and it / is important that you do not act without first informing / him. I want to make this absolutely clear so that / you will not be embarrassed, because it is certain that / we cannot come to the rescue of anyone. We are / not doing anything at once about reducing staff, and economies / now are better than something drastic next month. We have / had our fair share of problems but we have been / keeping an eye on costs and expenses. The steps taken / are for your own sake and although they are not / pleasant, they are necessary. I did not want you to / think that we have been hasty or that we have / been negligent in not advising you at once about developments. / I want to assure you that the prospects are better / than they may appear and I can see a return / to better times. It is certain that we cannot experience / anything worse than we have done in the last year. / (**180**)

UNIT 18 (*Page 85, First Course*)

1 The manager of the department store has decided to make an announcement to the entire staff about a bonus scheme. (**20**)
2 Your appointment as a secretary to the accountant will be announced on the firm's notice board. (**16**)
3 He voiced the resentment of many people at the announcement of the beginning of new experiments. (**16**)
4 It will be a big disappointment if we have a postponement but some important adjustments have to be made. (**19**)
5 The head of the department will make an announcement about the new appointment and the man or woman appointed will start work on Thursday. (**24**)

UNIT 18 (*Page 86, First Course*)

1 The annual canal race is unlikely to take place unless we have endless sunshine. (**14**)
2 An analysis of the annual figures shows that the numbers of unlicensed vehicles rose last year. (**16**)
3 It is unlikely that a departmental appointment will be made today unless we enlist the help of the supervisors. (**19**)
4 Ornamental lace is often made of nylon and you are strongly advised to use only mild detergent. (**17**)
5 Do not begin unloading until noon unless you hear that you may start earlier but that is unlikely. (**18**)

UNIT 18 (*Page 87, First Course*)

1 It is hardly likely that such a lovely place will actually survive the tourists. (**14**)

2 Apparently he is keenly aware of the dangers but unfortunately he does not care. **(14)**

3 Many things can be bought fantastically cheaply but it is exceedingly expensive to get to that country. **(17)**

4 Our price list is totally unrealistic and must be revised urgently. **(11)**

5 The densely populated areas will certainly need help but it may be given unwillingly. **(14)**

UNIT 18 *Short Form and Phrase Drill*

Most departments are being visited by the manager and particularly / the Sales Department, the Accounts Department and the Export Department. / We will have to take steps accordingly to ensure that / he will find each department in a good state. Particulars / of the visit will be made known to us this / week and we will be able to organise the work / so that he can see exactly how each unit operates. / This is particularly important because, as you know, the manager / has only been with this company a short time. We / will have an opportunity to raise many subjects during his / visit and each staff member who wishes something to be / discussed should let me have details immediately. This is the / first time we have had such an opportunity and I / suggest you should not be slow in making the most / of it. If you check your own department thoroughly I / am sure you will be able to come up with / some good ideas. Just as fast as we present ideas / the firm promises some form of response. **(177)**

UNIT 19 *(Page 90, First Course)*

1 At our meeting next week to discuss your request for / a post you will be questioned about the language course quoted in the reference. **(24)**

2 If you have the necessary qualities for this job, you will be requested to make quick visits to our offices abroad. **(21)**

3 I am sure that your language abilities are adequate and cannot be equalled, but you will also require training to know about the goods manufactured by this company. **(28)**

4 Many questions and enquiries will have to be dealt with quickly and adequately once the new business is established. **(19)**

5 Quite often it is quiet in the square and this adds to its quality as a desirable place in which to live. **(22)**

UNIT 19 (*Page 91, First Course*)

1 When a price is quoted you will be asked to accept the quote quickly. (**14**)
2 Where will you be living and what will be your new address? (**12**)
3 Why do you want to live elsewhere when you will have good opportunities here and a better train service than anywhere else? (**22**)
4 While we have adequate stocks you should be requesting what you require for the next quota. (**16**)
5 The car has white wheels and that is why it requires cleaning. (**12**)

UNIT 19 *Short Form and Phrase Drill*

We have enquired about language requirements for working abroad but / to my knowledge no one has even acknowledged our enquiries. / You will be required to have certain skills but accurate / details are hard to obtain. If we had one particular / office to which we could direct all our enquiries, perhaps / we should be able to get results. Do you know / of such a place? I shall be pleased to have / particulars soon because almost all the students will be leaving / next week. We can do little right now, but at / least some help will be better than none if we / are to deal with so many enquiries. Thank you for / anything you will be able to do for us. I / am quite sure your knowledge on this subject is far / greater than mine. (**133**)

UNIT 20 (*Page 94, First Course*)

1 As a favour we had offered to freeze the fruit for them on Friday but we are free to do it tomorrow if they wish. (**25**)
2 We shall have pleasure in measuring the fence for you during our leisure time on Friday. (**16**)
3 Have you forgotten that we offered in the advertisement a free measuring service to all the customers for our carpets? (**20**)
4 On your next visit to Africa try this different cream and forget about sunburn problems. (**15**)
5 The standard of the food at the Manor Hotel was only average but I have had favourable reports of the other hotel next door. (**24**)

UNIT 20 (*Pages 95–6, First Course*)

1 I gather the weather was not so good this summer on the farm. It recovered, however, in the autumn. (**19**)
2 The silver that is made at the Mint is only wafer-thin but it has the government stamp on it. (**20**)
3 The gold and silver trinkets from the shipwreck were discovered by our divers. (**13**)
4 If the weather is reasonable we shall be able to gather in the harvest sooner than we thought. (**18**)
5 Thank you for the offer. It will, however, be necessary to ask for government help sooner than Thursday. (**18**)

UNIT 20 *Short Form and Phrase Drill*

From all I hear of Commercial Industries Limited, it is / altogether satisfactory and as a businessman I feel certain that / we should buy shares before their prices rise any more. / It is certain there will be good trading figures for / this year although we do not know how much better / than last year's they will be. We did not buy / before because we had very little money, but now there / is spare cash and it is very much a case / of having nothing to lose since good returns on our / investment seem so certain. We have been doing very well / with our own business because we have worked together as / a team and there is no reason for us to / hold back on investment now. There is more than ever / before a chance of making satisfactory progress commercially and we / are very much aware of this so that we must / make the best arrangements possible for our business. (**158**)

UNIT 21 (*Pages 100–1, First Course*)

1 We are hopeful of seeing many different flowers which are especially beautiful at this time of the year. (**18**)
2 If he is travelling to that country he will have to obtain official approval from that government. (**17**)
3 I had to travel far to fulfil the special demands of that powerful group. (**14**)
4 One of the best facials you can make for yourself is with water, soap and a flannel. Partially soap your face and then finally rinse it with cold water. (**29**)
5 It is our philosophy to be helpful in both the initial and final stages of the agreement. (**17**)

UNIT 21 (*Page 102, First Course*)

1 This report reflects the marvellous progress we have made. (**9**)
2 Our rival in this town is marvellous at copying our styles and selling at lower prices. (**16**)
3 The naval officers of these powerful countries, although genial in manner, are known to be rivals. (**16**)
4 The Chairman said that his firm would publish the novel because if they did not do so one of their rivals would. (**22**)
5 Noise can be muffled and this is reflected in the recent work of aeroplane manufacturers. (**15**)

UNIT 21 *Short Form and Phrase Drill*

We shall have to enlarge our plant as early as / possible if we wish to become an influential manufacturer. As / soon as it is possible to make an announcement that / we are enlarging our premises there should be immediate approval / for the necessary finance, and as soon as we can / make satisfactory arrangements with the United States it is certain / there will be very much extra work for us from / them. Next month we shall be able to discuss the / proposed enlargement of our plant but it will take some / months before the full costs are known. However, as soon / as we have all the particulars, we shall finalize our / sales plans with the firms in the United States of / America. Before several months have elapsed we hope to see / tremendous progress. (**132**)

UNIT 22 (*Page 106, First Course*)

1 The wife of the executive retrieved the handkerchief and gave it to her husband. (**14**)
2 The representative had a rough cough and we had to forgive him for his poor delivery. (**16**)
3 Repetitive drilling of half a paragraph of shorthand will achieve positive results. (**12**)
4 His wife usually serves a digestive biscuit with the tea at the end of a brief meeting. (**17**)
5 The Manager always gives a vote of thanks on behalf of the administrative staff. (**14**)

UNIT 22 (*Pages 107–10, First Course*)

1 Profits of £7,000 reflect a healthy balance sheet and definitely deserve your approval. (**15**)
2 Roughly half of the relatives will each receive gifts of £2,000. (**13**)
3 The revised target of two million tons of coal by the end of the year will be achieved at 1800 hours on 21st December. (**25**)
4 Please serve that lady with half a pound of coffee and a box of toffee, and reserve eight gift packages to be collected at 9.00 am tomorrow morning by one of the prefects from the school. (**37**)
5 The ten defects in the photographic equipment will cost £500 to repair. (**14**)

UNIT 22 *Short Form and Phrase Drill*

You have no doubt heard that we are out of / stock of a number of parts in spite of the / lack of any type of industrial delay. It will be / difficult for us to cope with this sort of setback / but we shall be better off to reduce our manufacturing / instead of closing part of the factory. Staff who have / no work can be employed in any one of a / wide range of other jobs. We are thankful that this / shortage did not come any earlier because this difficulty would / have been much worse. As a member of a large / group of commercial manufacturers, it is certain that it will / not be long before some arrangements to supply these parts / will have to be made. Other companies which have stocks / of the spare parts we need may be able to / help us so you need have no fear that this / difficulty will last for very long. (**156**)

UNIT 23 (*Page 113, First Course*)

1 This is a reminder that all orders for our feathery materials have to be calculated in metres. (**17**)
2 Another interview will be arranged at some time in the near future. (**12**)
3 I understood that you received a letter yesterday afternoon, but as there was no signature on it you returned it to the sender. (**23**)
4 All these matters will be discussed after Easter which is much later this year, so I shall send you a reminder of the date and time of the meeting. (**29**)
5 I ordered a coat for my mother from the leather centre as a premature birthday gift. (**16**)

UNIT 23 (*Pages 114–15, First Course*)

1 We shall put in a tender for typewriters, tape recorders and refrigerators. (**12**)
2 I wonder if the painter takes all his pictures to the director of the Pointer Art Gallery? (**17**)
3 It would be kinder to render a further account for all the extra expenditure instead of telling people that we owe you money. (**23**)
4 The distributor of 'Victor' accelerators wonders if there is an unknown factor in the area who is dealing with all the orders. (**22**)
5 It will be a wonder if our winters ever become much colder than the one we experienced this year. (**19**)

UNIT 23 *Short Form and Phrase Drill*

I will be there in January for the winter sports / and I know there is going to be a good / time for all. I have been there before and I / think there is no better place. In your letter you / said that you will be arriving later than the rest / of the crowd because of transport difficulties. Is there not / some other way for you to travel? I am thankful / that I live so near. If there is no other / route for you I can be there to meet you / on the date you give in your letter. Will you / please telephone me, therefore, if there is to be any / change in your time of arrival? I know that we / shall have a wonderful holiday for there is no better / place in the world and we know there is every / chance of our having more than satisfactory weather. (**148**)

UNIT 24 (*Page 118, First Course*)

1 Will you put the motion to this meeting that we should send a mission from our International Marketing Division to sell our beauty aids and lotions to the fashion houses in New York who already buy from us? (**38**)
2 I mentioned to you that there is a pension scheme and you will be given a full explanation later. (**19**)
3 The activities of the fashion division of our international group were mentioned on television recently and attention was drawn to our summer fashions. (**23**)

4 The examinations of this national professional body should be brought to your attention. (13)
5 There is one omission in the list of solutions for that examination paper. (13)

UNIT 24 (*Page 119, First Course*)

1 Opticians and beauticians work together to produce fashionable glasses. (9)
2 Your co-operation would be appreciated in the collection of additional specimen sets of headed stationery. (15)
3 With the expansion of the education division, there will be more situations available. (13)
4 If you will follow my instructions on this occasion and turn left at the station, you will see an inscription on the wall which states that a famous magician once lived in the building next to our offices. (38)
5 I mentioned on several occasions that the post was pensionable, subject to three months probation on both sides, but he took no action. (23)

UNIT 24 (*Page 120, First Course*)

1 We have a selection of locations to offer you for the proposed factory, but you will have to make a decision soon. (22)
2 Only by election may a physician become a member of the association. (12)
3 It is necessary to have a true vocation and affection for this art before you make the decision to become a musician. (22)
4 The position of all the professional musicians within this organization is in a state of transition, and until we are in possession of the final report we can tell you nothing. (31)
5 A succession of fiction writers has left the country to avoid taxation. (12)

UNIT 24 (*Pages 121–3, First Course*)

1 It will be unnecessary to challenge the leadership of the party but I should be unhappy to lose your friendship as a result of this decision. (26)

2 There are many immovable objects in the museum so it is unnecessary to think about changing their locations. (**18**)
3 You must not regard good tyres as non-essential because it is illegal to drive with worn tyres. (**18**)
4 The non-delivery of the projector will result in Mary's lecture on 'Citizenship and Scholarship' being cancelled. (**17**)
5 Because he was an irresolute and inhuman character our meeting was most unsatisfactory. (**13**)

UNIT 24 *Short Form and Phrase Drill*

Information and literature about these corporations is readily available and / I think you should be giving this matter your immediate / attention. A large corporation is always ready to assist and / I know there is every hope of your getting all / the information you need without difficulty. You will be carrying / out a wonderful piece of research and you should be / able to gain much satisfaction from it. It may take / several months and so I will arrange for the work / you usually do to be covered by someone in your / department. Your attention, however, must also be given to the / January sale and therefore as soon as you feel it / is time to do so, you will have to get / together a team to make the necessary arrangements. There is / no doubt that you have some very good staff in / your own department.
(**143**)

UNIT 25 *(Page 127, First Course)*

1 The condition of the Secretary of this Company is continuing to give cause for considerable concern and we shall all contribute in order to send flowers to the hospital. (**29**)
2 Details about the conference should be completed soon and confirmation in writing will be sent to you. (**17**)
3 I shall have to confer with my fellow directors on a date convenient to them and listen to any comments they may wish to make. (**25**)
4 The constant noise is bound to continue and in consequence we shall have to complain. (**15**)
5 It is common knowledge that the controls should connect with the motor to form a contact. (**16**)

UNIT 25 *(Pages 128–9, First Course)*

1 We shall have to reconsider all the circumstances in this case but manufacture of the chemical will be discontinued. **(19)**

2 The flat is self-contained and I can certainly recommend it to you. **(13)**

3 This award is in recognition of the uncomfortable and trying . circumstances in which you have had to work. **(18)**

4 We recognise that mistakes are not uncommon and some orders are unfortunately dispatched incomplete. **(14)**

5 The heating was disconnected and it is not surprising that the place was uncomfortable. **(14)**

6 Your attitude to work is far from satisfactory and it must improve. **(12)**

7 There is no substitute for service and the success of this company throughout the world depends upon it. **(18)**

8 Training courses and conference facilities are available in institutes of technology all over the regions. **(15)**

9 Last year after the earthquake that man was destitute but with personal determination and government aid he has rebuilt his shop. **(21)**

10 We teach our students at the institute that there is no substitute for a positive attitude and in consequence most of them do well. **(24)**

UNIT 25 *Short Form and Phrase Drill*

We are confident that we shall continue to progress notwithstanding / the difficult trading conditions most large corporations are facing at / present. Such difficulties are very common today but at least / we are better off than many and for that we / should be thankful. Nevertheless, we cannot afford to wait for / good things to come to us. Instead of waiting for / the tide to turn we will all have to work / very much harder and turn it ourselves. As you know, / we have a Works Committee and this Committee has a / number of plans before it for consideration. You will have / the votes of all of the members and they will / consider your requirements and pay close attention to them. For / the first time in several years, and notwithstanding our many / difficulties, there is a feeling of unity and confidence. **(139)**

TRANSCRIPTION PRACTICE

1 Dear Sir, I am enclosing a cheque for 50p / as requested although I am unable to appreciate the necessity / for this. I have been in business myself for many / years and I know that from time to time minor / errors occur but I do not know of any firm / which would request immediate payment of such a small amount. / I have been a regular customer for many years and / at one time I was overcharged, but after drawing this / matter to your attention I simply requested an adjustment in / the price of my next purchase. Yours faithfully, **(98)**

2 Dear Sir, I am pleased to inform you that the / parcel from your warehouse arrived today and as far as / I can see from a casual inspection the goods are / totally satisfactory. Your staff had made a very thorough job / of the packing and although there appears to have been / some careless handling, I suspect by the firm of carriers, / the contents were none-the-worse for wear. Please arrange / for a copy of your new catalogue to be sent / as soon as it is printed. Thank you for your / good service. Yours sincerely, Victoria Lee. **(93)**

3 Dear Mr Edgar, I was very pleased to receive your / letter, for which I thank you, and I have pleasure / in enclosing my new card. My departure date is the 14th of next month. As director of the new Medical / Centre I will be ordering large quantities of new equipment / from you. In these days no-one can afford to / squander money, and therefore I trust that you will be / able to offer some form of discount and continue to / give your wonderful service. Do you have an agent in / that part of the world? If you have and we / do encounter any problems can I rely on him to / give good service? If not perhaps you will consider appointing / my new company as agents and distributors for your products. / Yours sincerely, A Henderson. **(134)**

4 Please arrange to have a set of Christmas tree lights, / stock model 648, delivered to Miss Frances Price, / address attached, and instruct the van driver to do this / today. Every endeavour must be made to ensure that this / customer receives the lights today or tomorrow together with a / set of instructions and a guarantee. You will see from / the attached correspondence that this company is not really responsible / but I think it is important to maintain the high / standards we have set over the years. Our branded goods / have a fine reputation and no other company is going / to frighten our customers away. (105)

5 Dear Sir, Thank you for the information which you have / been good enough to send me about investing in your / Society. In these difficult days anyone with a fixed income / needs to be looking for better alternatives when investing money. / The state of affairs in this country and in many / other parts of the world has brought about an inflation / rate which is excessive and which has defeated the whole / purpose of saving for one's retirement. Your rate of interest / for long-term deposits is attractive and, to my knowledge, / is as good as many and better than most other / societies. I believe I will be better off investing some / of my savings with you and I will call at / your new department next week.
Yours faithfully, (127)

6 I am pleased to note that you will be arranging / for the child's bicycle to be removed from window display / number 4 by the end of this week. This is / to fulfil an especially urgent request from a customer and / I am sure it can be done with a minimal / amount of inconvenience to your staff and it will be / in no way detrimental to the whole window display. There / will be no need to remove any of the fluorescent / tubes and it will be comparatively simple to replace the / bicycle with another large toy. Please attach a label to / the bicycle marked 'For Delivery to Miss Player' and our / despatch department will take care of the delivery. (118)

7 Memo from the Advertising Manager to the Sales Manager, subject Circular Letter, today's date:

Several hundred circular letters have been sent today and consequently / you should be ready to handle the requests for free / samples within the next few days. Realising we cannot afford / to squander our advertising budget I think it is unquestionable / that this form of promotion is invaluable. You will be / required to deal with approximately 5000 requests which is / 10 per cent of the total mailing. (67)

The Pitman 2000 Dictionary of English and Shorthand

Containing the shorthand outlines and meanings of over 75000 words, this invaluable work of reference includes a summary of the changes in the Pitman 2000 form of Pitman's Shorthand. American pronunciation and spelling is included with cross-referenced entries showing the differences.

216 × 138 mm/848 pages/Cased
ISBN 0 273 01618 0

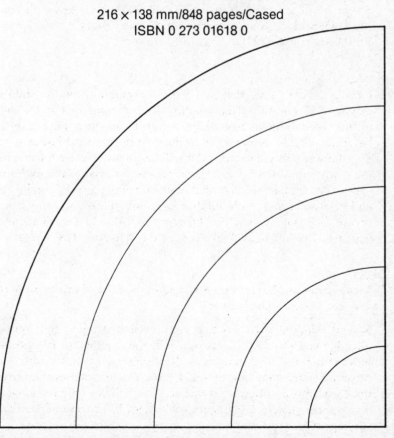